Literature for History–Social Science

Kindergarten Through Grade Eight

Prepared under the direction of the

**History–Social Science and
    Visual and Performing Arts Unit
California Department of Education**

Publishing Information

Literature for History–Social Science, Kindergarten Through Grade Eight was compiled by the History–Social Science and Visual and Performing Arts Unit, California Department of Education. It was edited for publication by Ralph Hanson and Bob Klingensmith, and it was prepared for photo-offset production by the staff of the Bureau of Publications. Juan Sanchez designed the cover and the interior layout, and Jeannette Huff set the type, with assistance from Merribeth Carlson and Carey Johnson. The document was published by the Department of Education, 721 Capitol Mall, Sacramento, California (mailing address: P.O. Box 944272, Sacramento, CA 94244-2720). It was printed by the Office of State Printing and distributed under the provisions of the Library Distribution Act and *Government Code* Section 11096.

Copies of this publication are available for $5.25 each, plus sales tax for California residents, from the Bureau of Publications, Sales Unit, California Department of Education, P.O. Box 271, Sacramento, CA 95812-0271.

A partial list of other publications available from the Department may be found on page 128, and a complete list may be obtained by writing to the address given above or by calling the Sales Unit at (916) 445-1260.

About the Cover

The cover of this document, which shows the *Mayflower* approaching the coast of Massachusetts in 1620, was reproduced from a colored steel engraving cut after a painting by a Boston artist, Marshall Johnson, around the turn of the twentieth century. The reproduction was used via an arrangement with, and publication rights were granted by, the Granger Collection, 1841 Broadway, New York, NY 10023.

ISBN 0-8011-0892-6

Contents

Foreword

Where there is history, children have transferred to them the advantages of old men; where history is absent, old men are as children.

> —*Juan Luis Vives, Sixteenth-century Spanish humanist*

A number of years ago, it was common for literate people to identify the books they owned with decorative bookplates. These bookplates were often a fascinating indication of the owner's personality or personal philosophy because they combined distinctive graphics, coats of arms, mottoes, or favorite quotations of the book's owner. One bookplate in particular is worth noting. It belonged to a child and sums up much of this document's principal message. The bookplate showed a view through a ship's porthole. In the distance could be seen a far horizon, a billowing sea, and an old sailing ship plowing the waves—a ship not unlike the one on this document's cover. Beneath this picture a moiré scroll displayed these words: *A book is a journey*.

The books listed in this document are journeys over centuries, transporting students to places and people distanced by time and space. Some of the journeys make an immediate and intimate impact on youngsters, giving them a vivid impression of what it was like to have been there, what was important to people then, why they acted as they did. Others offer a sense of detachment and allow a view from the perspective of hindsight. There are even a few sojourns within our own time, providing new discoveries that deepen students' understanding and empathy.

T. S. Eliot once noted a conspicuous trait among rising generations, that of a "new provincialism": the provinciality of time, binding youngsters to their own present moments. Little has been done since Eliot's day to counter this trait; in fact, the characteristic has become even more pronounced. The power and pleasure of story can help young people overcome this pointless limitation. Our future rests on their doing so.

It is my pleasure to introduce *Literature for History–Social Science, Kindergarten Through Grade Eight*. The works listed herein will assist teachers of history–social science and English–language arts, librarians, and curricular planners as they work to enrich the curriculum, as described in the *History–Social Science Framework for California Public Schools, Kindergarten Through Grade Twelve*. My best wishes for a rewarding and successful use of this resource.

Bill Honig

—*Bill Honig*
State Superintendent of Public Instruction

Preface

Hendrik van Loon, in *The Story of Mankind,* describes history as a *tower of experience* built out of the centuries. He portrays the vastness of this subject and observes the difficulties students sometimes have in mastering historical material. "It is no easy task to reach the top of this ancient structure and get the benefit of the full view," he writes. "There is no elevator, but young feet are strong, and it can be done."[1] *Literature for History–Social Science, Kindergarten Through Grade Eight* was prepared to help teachers and students to climb the tower together more easily and enjoyably.

Recent studies indicate that the use of historical fiction and biography can promote students' interest in and enthusiasm for studying history.[2] While the use of history-related literature in the classroom is by no means new, the *History–Social Science Framework for California Public Schools, Kindergarten Through Grade Twelve* emphasizes restoring the consistent use of this literature in the curriculum. Over the years, readings in historical literature give youngsters a fundamental grasp of earlier times and places and allow them to empathize with characters, events, and causes. But the rewards are to be reaped by more than students. Many teachers are discovering that literature sparks their own imaginations as they help students to discover the excitement of history and geography. The surest beginning that teachers can make toward framework implementation is to acquire a firsthand familiarity with the books that are appropriate for their grade levels.

New literary works are being written every day, and older titles are taken out of print almost as fast. Consequently, any reading list should be regarded as a "living document," a resource to be expanded as users discover additional appropriate titles. Further, *Literature for History–Social Science, Kindergarten Through Grade Eight* is not intended to be prescriptive, and school districts are encouraged to develop similar lists based on materials to which they have access.

Those who use this document will discover that some books listed as appropriate for one grade can be used at other levels as well. For example, several folktales listed for the first grade unit, "Developing Awareness of Cultural Diversity, Now and Long Ago," can also be used to complete the second grade study of family history and heritage; Marcia Sewall's *The Pilgrims of Plimoth* complements studies in the fifth grade as well as the third. Whatever the material, the course descriptions in the *History–Social Science Framework* are the bases for decisions. The books listed here support the objectives set forth in the framework's course descriptions; articulated selection is an important part of the curriculum coordination process.

---

1. Hendrik W. van Loon. *The Story of Mankind.* New York: Liveright, 1985, p. x.
2. *Theory and Research in Social Education,* Vol. 41, No. 1, pp. 1–15; also *Journal of Research and Development in Education,* Vol. 21, pp. 1–15.

As this document goes to press, most of the titles contained herein are obtainable from their publishers. In selecting works that complement units specified in the framework, however, the History–Social Science Model Curriculum Guide Advisory Committee did not exclude a book simply because it was no longer in print. The fact that a book is out of print is not necessarily a reflection of its intrinsic worth. Many excellent out-of-print titles are available through school libraries and public library search systems. Through inclusion of some that remain noteworthy for their treatments of a historical period and its people, ideas, and values, librarians and clerks are encouraged not to discard them from their collections. Finally, as in the case of *Recommended Readings in Literature, Kindergarten Through Grade Eight* (1986), it is hoped that publishers will be prompted to make certain titles available once more.

Among the books selected for each grade, a variety of reading levels are represented. Readability varies significantly within each grade so that students' varied interests can be accommodated. Also, teachers may choose to read particular works aloud and assign less difficult ones for independent and small-group reading. Suitability for the intended grade level, consistency with the strands and course content described in the framework, general quality and appeal—these were among the primary concerns of the advisory committee in reviewing books for this resource. While librarians and coordinators can offer invaluable assistance, the final decision in choosing books for classroom use rests with the teachers themselves.

Literature for History–Social Science, Kindergarten Through Grade Eight was more than a year in development. The document reflects numerous contributions from countless teachers, librarians, curriculum specialists, and booksellers who responded with suggestions after receiving preliminary drafts at the history–social science framework conferences in 1988. State Superintendent Bill Honig and the History–Social Science and Visual and Performing Arts Unit are grateful for the many recommendations and evaluations that were submitted during the preparation of this publication.

To all those who help youngsters discover through literature the excitement, passion, and depth in history's story, best wishes for a rewarding, remarkable, and limitless journey.

JAMES R. SMITH
Deputy Superintendent
Curriculum and Instructional Leadership Branch

FRANCIE ALEXANDER
Associate Superintendent
Curriculum, Instruction, and Assessment Division

TOMAS LOPEZ
Director
Office of Humanities Curriculum Services

DIANE L. BROOKS
Manager
History–Social Science and
Visual and Performing Arts Unit

Acknowledgments

The compilation of this book was led by the History–Social Science Model Curriculum Guide Advisory Committee, whose members included the following teachers, librarians, and curriculum specialists:

Zoe Acosta, Committee Chair
Office of the Kern County Superintendent of Schools

Rodney Atkinson
Office of the Kings County Superintendent of Schools

Bernice Barth
Hawthorne Elementary School
Beverly Hills Unified School District

Patricia Chavez
Wilson Elementary School
Colton Joint Unified School District

Jan Coleman
Thornton Junior High School
Fremont Unified School District

Lenore Daw
Fresno Unified School District

Rhoda Immer
Office of the Siskiyou County Superintendent of Schools

Amy Ish
El Gabilan Elementary School
Salinas City Elementary School District

Penny Kastanis
Office of the Sacramento County Superintendent of Schools

Steve Tietjen
Office of the Tulare County Superintendent of Schools

Ellis Vance
Clovis Unified School District

Appreciation is also extended to Mary Frances Donnelly Johnson of the Fresno County Public Library, Department of Readers' Services, for assistance in locating Spanish-language titles.

Supervision and support for the project were provided by staff of the Department of Education's History–Social Science and Visual and Performing Arts Unit: Diane L. Brooks, Manager; Rodney Atkinson, Consultant; Ira Clark, Consultant; Harvey N. Miller, Consultant; and Patty Taylor, Consultant.

Introduction

The *History–Social Science Framework for California Public Schools, Kindergarten Through Grade Twelve* calls for an integrated and correlated approach to the history–social science curriculum and stresses the importance of an engaging, lively narrative in the impartation of history's story. In the study of history and geography, literature is recommended as a particularly worthwhile means of generating students' interest, enhancing their understanding, and enriching the curriculum. The use of literature *of* the historical period being studied as well as *about* the period is emphasized. Consequently, *Literature for History–Social Science, Kindergarten Through Grade Eight* is offered as a resource of titles for use by curriculum specialists, teachers, librarians, and resource personnel when planning a curriculum.

Types of Literature

The term *literature* was used somewhat flexibly in the preparation of this document. This flexibility was necessary to compile a range of books that complement the course content described in the framework. Gail Gibbons's *The Post Office Book,* for example, is not thought of as literature in the same sense that one would think of Grimm's fairy tales, but it is a useful book for the first grade course. Similarly, letters and journals were not usually created for the purpose of literary art, but they are valuable literature for learning about earlier peoples and their times. As a result, a diversity of quality and intent may be seen in the listed materials. The brief explanation below gives some rationale for the inclusion of various literature types in this publication.

One of the most popular kinds of literature represented herein is *historical fiction*. Usually depicting the lives of ordinary people caught up in the circumstances and crises of particular times, such books are an effective means of developing a youngster's empathy for conditions during past eras. The best historical fiction incorporates characteristics of time and place so that they are vital to the story. Repeated encounters with good historical fiction establish images and impressions in the mind of the reader that form a more vivid sense of the past. As one reviewer observed, "Out of this maze of historical characters and intrigues and vignettes there will take shape in the young reader's imagination a glowing historical pattern, destined to endure far longer than the dry, bare-bones history taught in the typical social science classroom."

Biography is an especially powerful genre for young readers, not only for the light it sheds on the past but also for examples of human understanding. Lecturer and teacher Kay Goines once observed that biography and autobiography help youngsters form an answer to the question, "What is a life?" Reading of grand lives helps young people live humane, reasonable lives of their own. By reading about men and women, both ordinary and extraordinary, who made a difference, students develop a keener understanding of how human events result from human action. "History is nothing more nor less than biography on a grand scale," wrote Alphonse de Lamartine, and his statement emphasizes the importance of this genre to the history–social science discipline.

Fables are superb material for helping children think through the consequences of behavior. A fable is, as fantasist C. S. Lewis pointed out, a "supposal," a deliberate fiction intended to exemplify or impart a moral. The term *fable* originally meant "to give light," and that is exactly a fable's purpose: a short, sharp flash of insight into a potently ethical situation. The brevity of fables is ideal for their use with students who have short attention spans, and acting them out is a form of play that young children enjoy. For older students, fables can provide a deeper understanding of the cultures from which they sprang. Many popular expressions—e.g., "counting your chickens before they're hatched" and "crying 'wolf,' "—originated from fables. Acquisition of what is now called cultural literacy would be impossible without a mastery of the world's great fables.

Insight into a society's common memory and shared beliefs is similarly given by *myths* and *legends.* These works reflect how a people regarded the human condition, and because such stories often involve heroes and heroines, they demonstrate a people's self-concept and their sense of justice and duty. A close study of world myths can reveal commonalities as well as disparities between peoples. Tales of Zeus, Ra, Ulgen, and Ta-Aroa demonstrate that the human heart remains essentially the same over centuries and cultures.

Within the category of myths and legends are a number of legends based on actual figures in the history of the United States. Stories of George Washington and the cherry tree or Betsy Ross and the first flag may have a questionable base as history, but these tales develop in four-, five-, and six-year-olds common memories of persons whose real accomplishments require a more sophisticated background to appreciate. They familiarize children with historic names and events while encouraging interest in and fondness for them. In fact, they have an ethical benefit in that they provide insight into the nature of integrity, charity, and respect in the service of one's country. Homer did no less for the ancient Greeks. These legends should be enjoyed as mixtures of fact and fiction.

Ethics and values are further developed by the inclusion of *folktales* and *fairy tales* in the history–social science program. Though the relevance of the fey and fantastic to a curriculum supposedly dealing only with facts and issues is questioned at times, it is through such stories as "Rumpelstiltskin" and "Little Red Riding Hood" that the yearning for *lex talionis,* "the law of retribution," is satisfied and an early perception of justice is attained. Bruno Bettelheim, in *The Uses of Enchantment,* observed that many well-intentioned adults outlawed fairy tales for children "at just about the time when the findings of psychoanalysis made them aware that, far from being innocent, the mind of the young child is filled with anxious, destructive imaginings. . . . [These adults], so worried about not increasing a child's anxieties, remained oblivious to all the reassuring messages in fairy tales."[1] When chosen with care and presented in a nondidactic manner, fairy tales help foster moral perception through wonder and pathos, a credible part of the child's ethical and cultural heritage. A varied, more complete justification for this genre may be found in *Orthodoxy,* by G. K. Chesterton; *From Two to Five,* by Kornei Chukovsky; *Tree and Leaf,* by J. R. R. Tolkein; and Bettelheim's aforementioned book.

The *History–Social Science Framework* of 1988 calls for increased use of *primary sources.* Although technically not literature *per se,* print forms of primary sources appear throughout this document as a reminder to teachers and resource personnel of the importance of these sources in learning history. According to the Organization of American Historians, a primary source is any material generated at the "first level of experience"—eyewitness accounts, journals, diaries, firsthand testimony of events as they happened. Abraham Lincoln's "Gettysburg Address" could be used as a primary source because it is the text of historic words spoken at a historic moment. The power of primary source material—whether in original, facsimile, or transcribed form—is that it increases the user's sense of intimacy and immediacy with the past. It also gives authenticity to "second-level" accounts.

One of the distinguishing characteristics of the 1988 framework is the acknowledgment of religion's importance in history and the recognition that the history–social science curriculum should allow for teaching about religion in an appropriate context. In the second grade, for example, students are encouraged to share information about their families' religious practices to learn of the traditions and heritages reflected in family life. In the sixth and seventh grades, the religious heritages of Buddhism and Confucianism are studied in depth, as are portions from the Hebrew and Christian Bibles; e.g., the Exodus and Jesus' parables. Consequently, titles are included which reflect this content. The materials are not to be used for indoctrination but rather for learning about religion—its influence in history; its reflection of culture, values, and ideals; and its importance in the realm of human experience and action.

A range of *nonfiction* is included for the purposes of general interest, student research, and alignment with specific content in framework units. These titles can help form a nucleus of nontextbook library materials that support the framework's curriculum. A number of these books can serve as teachers' background material as well. Entries intended only for teachers' use are so indicated in the annotations.

As for *poetry, plays,* and *songs,* some of the most enduring examples of cultural heritage come from these categories. *Beowulf, The Rubaiyat,* the psalms of David, and haiku are examples from the wealth of world traditions; "Paul Revere's Ride,"

---

1. Bruno Bettelheim, *The Uses of Enchantment: The Meaning and Importance of Fairy Tales.* New York: Knopf, 1976, p. 122.

"Barbara Frietchie," "I, Too," "The Erie Canal," and "Over the River and Through the Wood" are all lasting samples from the cornucopia of American heritage. Curriculum planners should work with teachers in determining appropriate places for the use of such pieces so that students acquire a rich, common background over their school years.

Literature and Cultural Literacy

The development of a shared background in national heritage for all students is a major consideration in the selection of literature for the curriculum. In recent years, teachers and publishers have begun to highlight works by writers who previously had been unjustly neglected by many historians and educators; e.g., Phillis Wheatley, Frederick Douglass, and poetry of the American Indian heritage. As public awareness continues to grow, works by writers such as these become a part of our general cultural knowledge and understanding.

During the past 50 years, another group has suffered gradual neglect. Such authors as Washington Irving, James Fenimore Cooper, Nathaniel Hawthorne, Henry Wadsworth Longfellow, Louisa May Alcott, and Mark Twain used to be standard fare for American children, and their works helped to form a common cultural base for much of the nation. Every school child should have some familiarity with these writers. Though they may seem old-fashioned to some, many instructors find that certain selections can be exciting and rewarding to teach. Once youngsters get into such works as "Hiawatha's Childhood" and *Grandfather's Chair,* they begin to appreciate the people and cultures depicted. Content from the National Identity, Historical Literacy, Cultural Literacy, and Geographic Literacy strands, as identified in the *History–Social Science Framework,* can be learned from the works of these writers. They introduce students to the literary styles of earlier periods. The writings are rich, substantive, and deserving of a rightful place alongside those of more contemporary or diverse perspectives.

A most generous compendium of the writings that form the American heritage is *The American Reader, Words That Moved a Nation,* edited by Diane Ravitch (Harper Collins, 1990). Reflecting a broad diversity of thought and experience from over 200 years of United States history, selections include poems, songs, and inaugural addresses; essays by such writers as Ralph Waldo Emerson and Henry David Thoreau; John Brown's last statement before his execution; speeches and writings by Elizabeth Cady Stanton, Frederick Douglass, and David Waker; and a wealth of other varied literary works and primary sources.

Initial Planning

It would be impossible to cover all necessary history and geography in a given unit simply by having the class read literary works. In-depth studies encompass more.

Esther Forbes's *Johnny Tremain* can add immeasurably to students' understanding of the War for Independence, but other source material, technology, textbooks, and activities must be used to achieve a complete and essential picture.

Familiarity with literature is essential for teaching history-social science. Some years ago, in her book *Treasure for the Taking,* Anne Thaxter Eaton stressed that adults need to *read* rather than rely solely on reading lists such as this one. "Signposts on the highway are no substitute for a journey. By the same token, a list of books can be no substitute for firsthand acquaintance with the books themselves."[2]

Given an ongoing habit of reading, correlation of history–social science with other disciplines is the next important step toward successful integration of literature into the curriculum. Teachers with specialties in various subjects should work together with librarians and curriculum specialists so that curricular aims are accomplished. Teachers will want to consider some of the titles contained herein for "core" literature selections—those which are substantive, of proven and lasting worth, and significant in promoting historical and cultural literacy. The *History–Social Science Framework,* the three selection criteria described in the *Handbook for Planning an Effective Literature Program* (pp.16–18), and *Recommended Readings in Literature* (1986) provide a helpful base for selecting literature that enriches the teaching of history–social science and English–language arts.

Two departmental pamphlets for parents, *The Changing History–Social Science Curriculum* and *The Changing English–Language Arts Curriculum,* reinforce the importance of literature; the former contains sample titles that support these two subject areas.

Teaching with Literature

Reading aloud is one of the most important ways of introducing literature to students; however, despite many positive efforts, this practice is not yet a consistent feature at all grades. Noted author and columnist William F. Russell points out that a common mistake is to stop reading aloud to children once they have begun to read for themselves.[3] Even in departmentalized situations in middle and junior high schools, history–social science teachers can use a small portion of each class period for reading aloud works that enhance concurrent studies, leading students to make connections between what is heard and what is studied. Reading aloud sections of a work of literature is sometimes helpful in getting students to read independently. Some teachers intersperse reading aloud with small-group, whole-class, and individual reading so that lengthy or difficult works are more approachable.

---

2. Anne Thaxter Eaton, *Treasure for the Taking.* New York: Viking, 1957, p. ix.
3. William F. Russell, *Classic Myths to Read Aloud: The Classic Stories of Greek and Roman Mythology Specially Arranged by an Education Consultant.* New York: Crown, 1989, p. 1.

Literature can also be used effectively to supplement material found in textbooks. Passages from works by Jack London and Richard Henry Dana, for example, contain striking descriptions of the California coastline that can enhance fourth graders' study of California's geography. In the third grade, a brief storybook about the Liberty Bell can supplement the study of our national symbols. In this way, the history curriculum becomes *woven* with literature and refined with fine writing and narration.

To use literature effectively, teachers do not have to plan lengthy discussions of or activities for each work. Many shorter genres, picture books and poetry among them, pique interest and enhance understanding. Margaret Leaf's *Eyes of the Dragon* provides accent to the seventh grade unit on China and takes only a few minutes to share. A reading of Stephen Vincent Benet's "Ballad of William Sycamore" can link two eighth grade units, because the poem touches on the end of America's pioneer era as that era gave way to an industrial society. Often the "spell" of certain literary works makes the difference in students' enjoyment of history.

Integration efforts have sometimes included an approach termed "across the curriculum" or "webbing." Teachers must use this strategy with care to avoid trivializing the subject matter. There is a difference between integration that illumines the central meaning for students and integration which is merely associative. For example, to extend "The Ant and the Grasshopper" by launching a science unit on grasshoppers would miss the ethical and cultural literacy focus. The crux of a story's meaning must always be kept in mind in the planning of correlated activities.

Special Needs

Migrant education and Chapter 1 students (students who need special educational assistance as provided for by Chapter 1 of the Education Consolidation and Improvement Act of 1981) must be given equal access to a core curriculum rich with literature, history, and geography. These disciplines provide a depth of content that is ideal for instructing students who have special needs:

> For the language arts to function, they must be applied to some content. All students learn to listen by attending to that which edifies. They learn to talk not only by talking but also by talking about something substantive. They learn to read by reading something which engages their interest and fulfills a purpose and to write by composing that which records or clarifies.[4]

Trade book publishers are encouraged to realize the potential market for responsible, faithful translations of major works, making it possible for students to grasp content during initial steps toward English fluency. As this document goes to press, a mono-

---

4. *Effective Language Arts Programs for Chapter 1 and Migrant Education Students.* Sacramento: California Department of Education, 1989, p. 5.

graph dealing with special considerations for planning history–social science programs that meet diverse educational needs, including those of migrant education and Chapter 1 students, is being developed for distribution.

A Story Well Told

In his essay "History as a Humanistic Discipline," historian Gordon Craig describes the central role literature played in his historical understanding. As a student, Craig avoided history courses because of their "maddeningly dull" treatment. Nevertheless, Craig read historical fiction extensively, and his imagination was fired by such writers as G. A. Henty, Rudyard Kipling, and Sir Walter Scott. He gained no systematic knowledge of history by reading these authors, but their strong, exciting narratives offered accurate and picturesque detail, a sense of period, and a grasp of historical trends and social types. Even the romanticized aspects of these works fed Craig's fascination and gave him a background he would later alter and clarify.

Later, at Princeton University, Craig heard lectures by historian Walter Phelps Hall. The tide turned. This professor was able to achieve a sense of theater in his lectures, mixing suspense and humor with provocative visuals; Hall had even enthusiastically read some of the same literature which had meant so much to his young student. "He was . . . admirably persuasive in his insistence that history was so important and exciting that it required a total commitment from his auditors. . . . He taught history, in short, as a humanistic discipline."[5]

Craig's tribute testifies to the power of literature and imaginative teaching in conveying history's story. A book list such as this one suggests a wide range of potential resources to support instructional programs and offer choices to creative teachers. It is hoped that *Literature for History–Social Science, Kindergarten Through Grade Eight* finds a receptive, thoughtful audience eager to share an excitement for history and books with young people.

---

5. *Historical Literacy*. Edited by Paul Gagnon. New York: Macmillan, 1989, p. 123 ff.

Kindergarten:
Learning and Working,
Now and Long Ago

K.1   Learning to Work Together

Aesop. *The Aesop for Children.* Pictures by Milo Winter. Amereon Ltd., reprint of 1947 edition, or Checkerboard Press (Macmillan), 1984.

This book features brief stories with morals that have been told and retold for hundreds of years.

Almeida, Fernanda Lópes de. *La Margarita Friolenta.* Caracas: Ekaré (Colección Ponte-Poronte), n.d.; also SEP Libros del Rincón.

In this Spanish-language book, a child discovers that her plant needs love to stop its shivering.

Brett, Jan. *Goldilocks and the Three Bears.* Putnam, 1987.

The retelling of this traditional folktale is enjoyed by all children. See also Brett's *Beauty and the Beast* (Clarion, 1989).

Burningham, John. *Mr. Gumpy's Outing.* Holt, 1971.

Mr. Gumpy takes two children and an assortment of animals for a ride in his boat. The children do what they were warned not to do, the boat tips, and the consequences are predictable.

Cohen, Miriam. *See You Tomorrow, Charles.* Illustrated by Lillian Hoban. Greenwillow, 1983.

Charles is blind, and the other children try to protect him. But when they are locked in a dark basement, it is Charles who does the protecting.

Cox, David. *Tin Lizzie and Little Nell.* Random, 1989.

Winterbottom swears by his motor car, and Billy Beson believes avidly in his horse and sulky to provide transportation.

Curle, Jock. *The Four Good Friends.* North-South Books (Henry Holt), 1987.

This little-known folktale, delightful to children, features pastel-shaded illustrations.

DePaola, Tomie. *Pancakes for Breakfast.* Harcourt, 1978.

Through thinking and the help of others, a shortage dilemma is solved to the satisfaction of all concerned.

Dr. Seuss. *I Had Trouble Getting to Solla Sollew.* Random, 1980.

Through perseverance in overcoming hardships and with the cooperation of a variety of characters, the hero finally gets to Solla Sollew, but it isn't what he expects.

The Elves and the Shoemaker. Retold by Bernadette Watts. North-South Books (Holt), 1986.

This version of a Grimm's tale comes with large pictures by a leading illustrator. See also Watts's *Snow White and Rose Red.*

Flack, Marjorie. *The Story About Ping.* Viking, 1933.

Ping the duck explores a perilous but awesome world and learns to appreciate order and security, despite petty irritations.

Great Children's Stories: Classic Volland Edition. Illustrated by Frederick Richardson. Checkerboard Press (Macmillan), reprint of 1938 version.

This book presents a large, traditional collection of famous folktales and fairy tales.

Grimm, Jacob, and Wilhelm Grimm. *The Bremen-Town Musicians.* Retold and illustrated by Ilse Plume. Harper, 1987.

The mutual care and support the animals give each other in this story make this a favorite from the Grimm's cornucopia.

Hamilton, Virginia. *The People Could Fly.* Knopf, 1985.

This book contains 40 superb illustrations by Leo Dillon and Diane Dillon that add another level of vitality to an extraordinary collection of 24 tales that depict the black slaves' struggles for survival. These stories are best read aloud or told at this level.

Heine, Helme. *The Pearl.* Margaret K. McElderry (Macmillan), 1985.

This is a warm, fablelike story that demonstrates important values in living together. See also Heine's

Friends (same publisher, 1986). Both stories are also available in paperback.

The Helen Oxenbury Nursery Story Book. Retold by Helen Oxenbury. Knopf, 1985.

Oxenbury's collection of fairy stories is suitable for this grade level. Her *Working* (Simon and Schuster, 1981), is enjoyed by early kindergartners.

Heuer, Margarita. *El Zapato y el Pez.* Mexico City: Trillas, 1983.

This title (The shoe and the fish) joins Heuer's *Hercules y la Chispa* and *Lucecita* (same publisher) as Spanish-language stories suitable for this unit.

Hutchins, Pat. *The Doorbell Rang.* Greenwillow, 1986.

This book presents a lighthearted way to introduce the ramifications of scarcity.

Jack and the Beanstalk. Illustrated by Paul Galdone. Clarion, 1982.

The famous story of courage and perspicacity is retold by a favorite illustrator. Galdone's *Little Red Hen* and *Three Little Pigs* are also enjoyed by children.

Los Tres Osos y Bucles de Oro. Illustrated by Gloria Carasusan. Barcelona: Juventud, 1977.

This is a Spanish translation of *Goldilocks and the Three Bears.*

Parsons, Ellen. *Rainy Day Together.* Illustrated by Lillian Hoban. Harper, 1971.

This is a charming portrait of a little girl and her mother on a rainy day. They share chores, games, and meals, and Daddy comes home to make the day complete.

Robart, Rose. *The Cake That Mack Ate.* Little, Brown, 1987.

The value of sharing can be related to this little story of farm life.

Rockwell, Anne. *The Three Sillies and Ten Other Stories to Read Aloud.* Harper, 1986.

This is a collection of well-known tales retold and delightfully illustrated in bright colors.

Rogers, Fred. *Making Friends.* Putnam, 1987.

Mr. Rogers's gentle, empathetic nature and conver-

sational style are fully evident here in two books that are reassuring to young children. See also *Moving* (Putnum, 1987) by the same author.

Roland, Donna. *More of Grandfather's Stories from the Philippines.* San Diego: Open My World Publishing, 1985.

This publisher issues folktales of other ethnic origins as well.

Rumpelstiltskin. Retold by Paul Zelinsky. Dutton, 1986.

This edition of the Grimms' tale is a Caldecott Award–winner. See also Galdone's version (Clarion, 1982).

Siebert, Diane. *Truck Song.* Illustrated by Byron Barton. Harper, 1984.

A rhymed text complements the brilliantly colored drawings in this book and takes the child on a transcontinental journey in a truck.

Stevens, Janet. *Androcles and the Lion.* Holiday, 1989.

This is an illustrated version of the classic Aesop story. See also Stevens's *Goldilocks and the Three Bears.*

Tolstoi, Alexi. *The Great Big Enormous Turnip.* Watts, 1968.

It takes more than just one person to pull a giant turnip out of the ground, so the farmer calls on his family and friends to help.

Tusquets, Esther. *La Conejita Marcela.* Barcelona: Lumen, 1980.

This book features Marcela, the little rabbit. It is written in Spanish.

Wells, Rosemary. *Shy Charles.* Dial, 1988.

This delightful author reaches youngsters, and teachers should review other titles of hers, such as *Timothy Goes to School* and *Noisy Nora. Julieta, Estate Quieta* is a Wells book in Spanish translation. (México: Libros del Rincón, 1989; Spain: Altea, Colección Benjamín, n.d.).

Williams, Vera B. *Music, Music for Everyone.* Greenwillow, 1984.

This book incorporates several of the values and facets of this unit: cooperation, communication, and problem solving. The ethnically mixed neighborhood in the story is a happy feature of this book.

K.2 Working Together: Exploring, Creating, and Communicating

Barton, Byron. *Machines at Work.* Harper, 1987.

The brief text of this book, complemented by brilliantly colored graphics, describes what happens from the time the passenger arrives at the airport until the plane is airborne. See also Barton's *Airport* (Harper, 1987).

Brown, Margaret Wise. *The Important Book.* Harper Junior, 1949.

To recognize attributes of persons and places is critical for a deeper understanding of the world around us. This little book can be supplemented with *Where Have You Been?* (Hastings reprint, 1986).

Crews, Donald. *School Bus.* Greenwillow, 1984.

This is an account of the progress of school buses as they take children to school and bring them home again.

Goffstein, M. B. *A Writer.* Harper Junior, 1984.

Teachers should review *A Little Schubert, An Actor,* and *An Artist* by the same author. These books clarify the special qualities of these communicators.

Hazen, Barbara Shook. *Even If I Did Something Awful.* Atheneum, 1981.

Afraid that breaking a favorite vase will destroy her mother's love, a little girl asks questions about imaginary misdeeds.

Kightley, Rosalinda. *The Postman.* Macmillan, 1988.

This volume and its companion, *The Farmer,* are simple and cheerful depictions of human activity in community life.

Lenski, Lois. *The Little Auto.* McKay, 1980.

This memorable book is part of the old Mr. SMALL series. See also Lenski's *The Little Airplane, The Little Train,* and *The Big Book of Mr. Small.* These books are somewhat dated but still appealing.

Lionni, Leo. *It's Mine.* Knopf, 1986.

A fanciful, brightly illustrated fable in which three quarrelsome frogs learn to cooperate and share is told in this book. See also *Swimmy* and *Fish Is Fish* by the same author.

Lobel, Arnold. *Frog and Toad Are Friends.* Harper, 1970.

This is one of a series of books about friendship, cooperation, and the adjustments friends make for each other. The value of friendship is emphasized in this book.

Provensen, Alice. *Town and Country.* Crown, 1985.

This book describes life in a big city and on a farm near a village.

Sendak, Maurice. *Pierre.* Harper Junior, 1962.

A recalcitrant youngster learns the importance of caring. This humorous story is written in verse.

Steptoe, John. *Stevie.* Harper, 1969.

Robert, an only child, tells the story of Stevie, who is younger, who comes to live with him and upsets everything. But when Stevie leaves, the house is so empty.

K.3 Reaching Out to Times Past

Adler, David A. *A Picture Book of George Washington.* Holiday, 1989.

This picture book presents a biography of the commander-in-chief of the Continental army and first president of the U.S. The book has as its companion Adler's *A Picture Book of Abraham Lincoln.*

Aliki. *Go Tell Aunt Rhody.* Macmillan, 1986.

The American folk song from which this story is derived depicts a way of life from the late 1800s. This picture story overcomes the somewhat mournful quality of the song.

Allen, Thomas B. *On Granddaddy's Farm.* Knopf, 1989.

The agrarian way of life is lovingly recalled in this personal recollection of times past. Used in this unit, the book presents an opportunity for developing historical empathy.

Anderson, Joan. *The First Thanksgiving Feast.* Clarion, 1984.

This is a photo account of the 1621 harvest feast celebrated by the Pilgrims, using actors and the seventeenth-century setting of Plimoth Plantation, a living museum in Plymouth, Massachusetts.

Azarian, Mary. *A Farmer's Alphabet.* David R. Godine, 1981.

This is a noteworthy picture book depicting an older, agrarian way of life. Teachers can show the hard-back version and cut and laminate the paperback version for display.

Bulla, Clyde Robert. *Daniel's Duck.* Harper, 1979.

Daniel is hurt when others laugh at his wood carving, but then he learns that giving people pleasure takes a very special gift.

Carrick, Carol. *Patrick's Dinosaurs.* Clarion, 1985.

When his brother talks about dinosaurs, Patrick is afraid until he finds out they all died millions of years ago.

Dragonwagon, Crescent. *Home Place.* Macmillan, 1990.

Half a chimney covered with vines is all that is left of a family home of long ago. In this book, the narrator and illustrator permit us to hear the voices and envision the lives of the hardy people who once lived in the house now gone.

Field, Rachel. *General Store.* Greenwillow, 1988.

Illustrations by Nancy Winslow Parker make possible a comparison with the modern-day super-market.

Gerrard, Roy. *Sir Cedric.* Farrar, 1984.

Round-headed, short-bodied knights and ladies and the intricate patterns, detailed landscapes, and authentic castles in this picture book about medieval days will please any child. The romantic tale of Sir Cedric and his sweet Matilda is told in rollicking rhyme.

Giovanni, Nikki. *Spin a Soft Black Song.* Farrar, 1985.

This is a beautifully illustrated book of poems about the childhoods of blacks and about growing up as seen through the eyes of the very young.

Greene, Carol. *Benjamin Franklin: A Man with Many Jobs.* Children's Press, 1988.

The illustrations in this book are authentic and of primary interest.

Greenfield, Eloise. *Honey I Love and Other Poems.* Crowell, 1978.

This is a slim volume of poetry from the black American heritage. Many of its poems are short and appealing to young children.

Hale, Sarah Josepha. *Mary Had a Little Lamb.* Holiday, 1984.

Children will enjoy this familiar story, beautifully illustrated in a nineteenth-century mood. This book includes six stanzas of the original poem, the melody, and some historical context.

Hall, Donald. *The Ox-Cart Man.* Illustrated by Barbara Cooney. Viking, 1979.

The lovely fragility of a way of life now gone is depicted in this book. The rhythmic sequence of production and trade is conveyed so that the poetry in mundane life is evident.

Hodges, Margaret. *The Firebringer: A Paiute Indian Legend.* Little, Brown, 1972.

This is a thoughtful, authentic story with illustrations by Peter Parnall. It deserves republication.

Howard, Elizabeth Fitzgerald. *Chita's Christmas Tree.* Bradbury, 1989.

Set in Baltimore in the early twentieth century, Howard's story tells of the daughter of one of the city's first black doctors.

Hunt, Jonathan. *Illuminations.* Bradbury, 1989.

Though some of the material in this medieval alphabet is too sophisticated for six-year-olds, the pictures can generate real curiosity about older times. Teachers should select pages and passages to share.

Langstaff, John. *Hot Cross Buns and Other Old Street Cries.* Atheneum, 1978.

This book is a collection of old English street cries

used by strawberry sellers, knife grinders, and others selling their wares. These were the "commercials" of their day, and children enjoy singing and acting them out. This book is back in print.

McDermott, Gerald. *Arrow to the Sun.* Viking, 1974.

In this Pueblo Indian tale, the Lord of the Sun sends a spark to earth. The spark becomes a boy who searches for his father. This brilliantly illustrated tale shows the Indians' reverence for the sun.

McKissack, Patricia. *Mirandy and Brother Wind.* Knopf, 1988.

This charming picture book incorporates the famous cakewalk dance in its reflection of Afro-American life early in this century. If read aloud to children at this grade level, it can be enriched with singing games from the American black tradition.

Monjo, F. N. *The Secret of the Sachem's Tree.* Dell, 1973.

One of Connecticut's cherished legends is the basis for an absorbing story of early colonial days when many plans are brewing for events that will take place on Halloween.

Nashone. *Where Indians Live: American Indian Houses.* Sierra Oaks Publishing Co., 1989.

Photographs and sketches illustrate this discussion of Indian shelters, heroes, and culture.

Parish, Peggy. *Let's Be Early Settlers with Daniel Boone.* Harper, 1967.

This book is a teacher's resource. The many crafts and activities described herein—costumes, models, everyday items—will trigger ideas to help kindergartners develop historical empathy.

Quackenbush, Robert. *Don't You Dare Shoot That Bear!* Simon and Schuster, 1984.

This is a humorous biographical introduction to the first Teddy—Roosevelt, that is.

Spier, Peter. *The Legend of New Amsterdam.* Doubleday, 1979.

This is a lively excursion into early America to visit the settlers of what is now New York. It includes the author-artist's pictures as a guide.

Turkle, Brinton. *Thy Friend, Obadiah.* Viking, 1969.

Obadiah is a little Quaker boy living in old Nantucket. This book offers a delightful picture of a sensitive little boy who learns about being a friend. See also *Adventures of Obadiah* and *Obadiah the Bold* by the same author.

van der Meer, Ron, and Dr. Alan McGowan. *Sailing Ships.* Viking, 1984.

The artwork in this pop-up book invites students to act out life on the high seas in the days of sailing ships.

Van Woerkom, Dorothy. *Becky and the Bear.* Putnam, 1975.

A young girl in colonial Maine manages to catch a bear in an unusual way.

Visiting Grandma. Illustrated by Ernest Nister. Putnam, 1989.

Nister was one of the outstanding illustrators of the Victorian era, and his work appears here as a pop-up book. Scenes of childhood in earlier times recall past joys: apple tree swings, wheat gathering, holidays. Nister's *Special Days* (Putnam) is a companion volume. The illustrations are matched with evocative verse.

Weil, Lisa. *Let's Go to the Museum.* Holiday, 1989.

Visiting a museum is a wonderful way to reach out to times past. This book can be students' first contact with historic terms and places.

Wilder, Laura Ingalls. *Little House in the Big Woods.* Harper, 1953.

This is the autobiographical story of a pioneer family in Wisconsin in the 1870s. Excerpts can be read to kindergartners.

Wright, Blanche Fisher. *The Real Mother Goose.* Rand McNally, 1983.

Popular nursery rhymes are retold in this book. See also the Classic Volland Edition illustrated by Frederick Richardson (Rand McNally, 1971).

Grade One:
A Child's Place
in Time and Space

1.1 Developing Social Skills and Responsibilities

Aardema, Verna. *Bimwili and the Zumwi.* Dial, 1985.

Bimwili's first trip to the sea is filled with wonders good and bad. This tale resounds with the emotions of childhood, which are richly reflected in the illustrations.

Aesop. *Aesop's Fables.* Illustrated by Walt Sturrock. Unicorn Press, 1988.

A few of these tales can supplement those in the Checkerboard Press's edition (see the kindergarten listings).

Barnes, Beatriz. *La Cigarra y la Hormiga.* Illustrated by Marta Gaspar. México: Libros del Rincón, SEP (Cuentos de Polidoro), 1968, 1989.

A Spanish translation of the fable of the ant and the grasshopper is related here. See also *La Lechera y el Cántaro* (The milkmaid and her pail), available from the same publisher.

Beskow, Elsa. *Pelle's New Suit.* Harper, 1989.

A reprinted classic, this picture book shows community and cooperation in the making of new clothes for a youngster.

Burton, Virginia Lee. *Katy and the Big Snow.* Houghton, 1974.

This is a modern classic of a hard worker whose job takes her here and there and around the town. See also this author's *Mike Mulligan and His Steam Shovel* (Houghton Mifflin, 1967).

Caudill, Rebecca. *Did You Carry the Flag Today, Charlie?* Holt, 1966.

Each day one child is chosen to lead the boys and girls to the bus and carry the flag. This is the story of how Charlie finally came to carry the flag.

Cazet, Denys. *A Fish in His Pocket.* Watts, 1987.

A sensitive little bear accidentally causes a fish to die and conceives of a fitting farewell to it. Few picture books demonstrate as strong a respect for life as this one does.

Cohen, Miriam. *Starring First Grade.* Greenwillow, 1985.

A delightful class plans a play, but problems arise when Jim doesn't get the part he wants. Friendship wins the day, and the play is a success.

Conford, Ellen. *Impossible Possum.* Little, Brown, 1971.

This funny, shrewd tale of diligence and application can be found in many libraries.

Cooney, Barbara. *Miss Rumphius.* Viking, 1982.

This is the story of a lady who sets out to make the world more beautiful and does so by planting lupines.

Delamar, Gloria. *Play Aesop.* Eldridge Publishing Co., 1971.

This work is a handy resource of short skits in rhyme.

El Campo y la Ciudad. México: Editorial Patria (Colección Piñata), 1985.

A comparison of city and country life is depicted here in Spanish.

The Fables of La Fontaine. Translated by Lisa Commager. Exeter Books (Simon and Schuster), 1985.

The French fabulist's work is given good prose translation here.

Gag, Wanda. *Gone Is Gone.* Putnam, 1960.

This book presents a delightful folktale with a wry message. Fritzl learns never to take Liesi's work for granted.

The Hare and the Tortoise. Illustrated by Paul Galdone. McGraw-Hill, 1962.

This is a simple version of the Aesop fable.

Heyer, Marilee. *The Weaving of a Dream: A Chinese Folktale.* Viking, 1986.

A poor widow weaves her dreams into a beautiful

brocade and will die of grief if her three sons are unable to recover her treasure from the fairies who stole it.

Hoban, Russell. *Bargain for Frances.* Illustrated by Lillian Hoban. Harper, 1970.

Frances thinks she will heed her mother's warning and "be careful" as she goes to play with her friend Thelma. Various complications lead Frances to conclusions about the importance of friendship.

Hoguet, Susan Ramsay. *Solomon Grundy.* Dutton, 1986.

Solomon Grundy is a nursery-rhyme character whose life echoes the days of the week. This story makes Solomon a part of the immigrant experience and the growth of America.

Hort, Lenny. *The Boy Who Held Back the Sea.* Illustrated by Thomas Locker. Dial, 1987.

This fine old Dutch tale is suitable for reading aloud. It depicts a young boy's perspicacity and initiative. Features of geography are depicted in Thomas Locker's rich pictures, and the story provides opportunities for reflection and discussion.

Howitt, Mary. "The Spider and the Fly," in *Favorite Poems Old and New.* Edited by Helen Ferris. Doubleday, 1957.

This cautionary tale is a vivid portrayal of evil flattery. Despite the level of its language, young children can easily follow its meaning when it is read interpretively (with visuals), discussed, and enacted.

Kuskin, Karla. *The Philharmonic Gets Dressed.* Harper, 1982.

"Their work is to play," and how they work together!

Lobel, Arnold. *Fables.* Harper, 1980.

These are humorous, contemporary fables.

McGuffey, William Holmes, et al. *McGuffey's Third Eclectic Reader* (Revised edition). Van Nostrand Reinhold (reprinters of the 1879 version).

Sprinkled throughout this classic reader are gems still usable today for discussing ethics and values.

Ness, Evaline. *Sam, Bangs and Moonshine.* Holt, 1966.

Sam is a lonely little girl who lives in a fantasy world. Her lack of concern for reality almost causes the death of a playmate and a beloved pet.

Rylant, Cynthia. *When I Was Young in the Mountains.* Dutton, 1982.

The simple text of this book tells of a child's remembrances of other pleasures of life in the mountains of Appalachia. The warmth of family life is revealed through the story and beautiful illustrations.

Steig, William. *Amos and Boris.* Farrar, 1971.

A famous tale of friendship and duty.

Szilagyi, Mary. *The Adventures of Charlie and His Wheat-Straw Hat.* Putnam, 1986.

Seven-year-old Charlie helps his grandmother make a straw hat and then defends it from Confederate soldiers. Responsibility and devotion to tasks are shown in this story.

Tejima, Keizaburo. *Fox's Dream.* Translated from Japanese by Susan Matsui. Philomel (Putnam), 1987.

The cycle of life is revealed through the loneliness of a solitary fox in winter. With its poetic text and startling icy images, this is the perfect book for story hours and reflective times.

1.2 Expanding Children's Geographic and Economic Worlds

Baker, Jeannie. *Where the Forest Meets the Sea.* Greenwillow, 1988.

This book is recommended for the way land and sea features are described.

Bell, Neill. *The Book of Where: Or How to Be Naturally Geographic.* Little, Brown, 1982.

The text, illustrations, and suggested activities included in this book outline such basic concepts of geography as scale, map, globe, continental plates, and oceans. A useful teacher's resource.

Bemelmans, Ludwig. *Quito Express.* Viking, 1965.

Little Pedro has an unexpected adventure when a famous train rolls through his village in Ecuador.

Gibbons, Gail. *The Post Office Book: Mail and How It Moves.* Crowell, 1982.

Gibbons has a knack for making complicated things plain to children. See also *Fill It Up, Department Store, New Road!,* and other works by this prolific author.

Gramatky, Hardie. *Little Toot.* Putnam, 1959.

A little tugboat grows up by learning a hard lesson.

Gross, Ruth Belov. *Money, Money, Money.* Scholastic, 1971.

This book provides a brief history of barter and trade and the growth of these systems into a monetary system that includes metal coins, paper, and plastic.

Knowlton, Jack. *Geography from A to Z: A Picture Glossary.* Crowell, 1988.

This well-illustrated book is centered on geographic themes.

Krementz, Jill. *A Visit to Washington, D.C.* Scholastic, 1987.

On a tour of our nation's capital, six-year-old Matt Wilson, his brother Cole, and their parents show the reader the best places to visit in Washington, D.C.

Lobel, Arnold. *On Market Street.* Greenwillow, 1981.

This beautifully illustrated picture book describes a shopping trip. Each illustration is a figure made of the item being purchased.

Maestro, Betsy, and Ellen Del Vecchio. *Big City Port.* Macmillan, 1983.

This book clarifies for children how a port works. Geographic and economic elements are incorporated.

Rettich, Margret. *Suleiman the Elephant.* Lothrop, 1986.

Suleiman the elephant was a wedding gift to Prince Max of Austria and Princess Maria of Spain from the king of Portugal. The humorous text and full-color illustrations in this book capture the pageantry of Suleiman's journey from Spain to Vienna in 1551.

Schwartz, David M. *If You Made a Million.* Lothrop, 1989.

Beautiful illustrations and simple text introduce

students to monetary concepts. See also Schwartz's earlier book, *How Much Is a Million?* (1985).

Spier, Peter. *Tin Lizzie.* Doubleday, 1978.

Peter Spier tells the nostalgic story of one of the favorite symbols of America, the Tin Lizzie, a 1901 Model T touring car.

Swift, Hildegard. *The Little Red Lighthouse and the Great Gray Bridge.* Harcourt, 1974.

A real little red lighthouse is placed in the shadow of the great George Washington Bridge, which spans the Hudson River. Through this tale, we better comprehend our place in the world.

Viorst, Judith. *Alexander Who Used to Be Rich Last Sunday.* Atheneum, 1980.

This is the story of how Alexander and the dollar that his grandparents gave him are soon parted. He feels rich until it is quickly gone.

Willard, Nancy. *The Voyage of the Ludgate Hill: Travels with Robert Louis Stevenson.* Illustrated by Alice Provensen and Martin Provensen. Harcourt, 1987.

In this book, based on Stevenson's Atlantic crossing, Willard's buoyant verse tells of the people—as well as the monkeys, horses, and goats—who traveled on the cargo steamer.

1.3 Developing Awareness of Cultural Diversity, Now and Long Ago

Aardema, Verna. *Bringing the Rain to Kapiti Plain.* Dial, 1981.

This retelling of a tale from Kenya employs a cumulative style to tell of animals in a drought. See also *Why Mosquitoes Buzz in People's Ears: A West African Tale* (Dial, 1978) by the same author.

Agard, John. *The Calypso Alphabet.* Holt, 1989.

Words presented alphabetically in this book with scratchboard illustrations entice students to consider island culture.

Alexander, Ellen. *Llama and the Great Flood: A Folktale of Peru.* Crowell, 1989.

A llama saves people from a flood by leading them to safety. This is a tale from the Andes, and the author's notes provide a helpful background.

Alexander, Sue. *Nadia the Willful*. Pantheon, 1983.

Set against a backdrop of the Arabian desert, the story tells of a girl's determination in overcoming the loss of her brother.

Al-Saleh, Khairat. *Fabled Cities, Princes and Jinn from Arabic Myths and Legends*. Schocken Press, 1985.

This collection of stories stemming from Arabian and Persian traditions is usable at more than one grade level. Some selections are better told to children at this grade level.

Anno, Mitsumasa. *All in a Day*. Putnam, 1986.

This brief text and the illustrations by ten internationally known artists reveal a day in the lives of children in eight different countries. The similarities and differences in the lives of these children emphasize the commonality of humankind.

Baylor, Byrd. *Hawk, I'm Your Brother*. Macmillan, 1976.

A young Indian steals a baby hawk because he thinks he will learn to fly if the hawk is his brother. The boy frees the hawk when he finds it is not happy in captivity.

Behrens, June. *Fiesta! Ethnic Traditional Holidays*. Children's Press, 1978.

This book provides an introduction to the Mexican holiday that commemorates the victory of the Mexican army over the French in 1862, a victory that signaled the end of foreign invasion of North America.

Bess, Clayton. *Truth About the Moon*. Houghton, 1983.

This is a charming tale of a West African child with insatiable curiosity. It intermingles folklore with a contemporary story that children will enjoy hearing again and again.

Carasusan Ballve, Gloria. *Yaci y Su Muñeca*. Barcelona: Juventud (Colección Kukuruku), 1974.

This Spanish-language book presents an authentic story of Brazilian life.

Carpenter, Frances. *Tales of a Korean Grandmother*. C. E. Tuttle, 1972 (reprint of a 1937 edition).

This is a superb collection of valuable material—folktales collected from many sources and beautifully illustrated with old Korean paintings.

Ching Hou-Tien. *The Chinese New Year*. Holt, 1976.

Chinese New Year is a festive and elaborate holiday. This book, illustrated with the ancient Chinese art of paper cutting, is a delightful introduction to the pageantry and ritual of this five-day celebration.

Climo, Shirley. *The Egyptian Cinderella*. Crowell, 1989.

This authentic fable of ancient Egypt shows marked similarities to the story of Cinderella. The author tells the tale for young audiences, and the illustrations depict life during the time of the pharaohs.

Cooney, Barbara. *Chanticleer and the Fox*. Crowell, 1958.

Adapted from Chaucer's "Nun's Priest's Tale" of the *Canterbury Tales,* this fable allows students to reflect on the deceit of flattery.

Costabel, Eva Deutsch. *The Pennsylvania Dutch: Craftsmen and Farmers*. New York: Atheneum, 1986.

The crafts of the Pennsylvania Dutch living in a rural atmosphere are described in this book. Included are quilting, pottery, tinware, and tableware.

Courtalon, Corinne. *On the Banks of the Pharaoh's Nile*. Young Discovery Library, 1988.

The *Young Discovery* series is attractive but small-sized. First graders will not be able to read the text by themselves, but the illustrations, with explanations, can introduce youngsters to diverse cultures of the past. See also *Following Indian Trails, Long Ago in a Castle,* and *Living in India* from the same series.

Craft, Ruth. *The Day of the Rainbow*. Viking, 1989.

The ethnic diversity of big-city life is reflected in this lost-and-found story set in midsummer.

De Armond, Dale. *The Seal Oil Lamp*. Little, Brown, 1988.

A seven-year-old Eskimo boy is left to die because his blindness will make him a burden to the village. Black-and-white woodcuts portray Eskimo life in harmony with nature.

Demi. ***Dragon Kites and Dragonflies: A Collection of Chinese Nursery Rhymes.*** Harcourt, 1986.

This is an illustrated collection of 22 traditional Chinese nursery rhymes. "Two Peacocks" from *Demi's Reflective Fables* (Putnam, 1988) is also usable.

DePaola, Tomie. ***The Legend of the Indian Paintbrush.*** Putnam, 1988.

Little Gopher, who uses his special gift to record his people's history on painted animal skins, finally achieves his "dream-vision" of capturing on canvas the color of the sunset. See also *The Legend of the Bluebonnet* and *Tony's Bread* by the same author.

Durkán Sapuana, Dalia. ***Somos Guajiros.*** Photos by Alex Dearden and Mauricio Martínez. Caracas: Ekare (Colección Gente Nuestra), 1988.

This is a Spanish-language account of the daily life of the Sapuana clan in the Guajira area of Venezuela and Colombia.

Feelings, Muriel, and Tom Feelings. ***Jambo Means Hello: Swahili Alphabet Book.*** Dial, 1974.

This alphabet book is noteworthy for its presentation of a culture most students will find unusual.

Flora. ***Feathers Like a Rainbow: An Amazon Indian Tale.*** Harper, 1989.

Geographic features underlie this folktale of how the birds of the rain forest got their bright colors.

Foster, Sally. ***Where Time Stands Still.*** Putnam, 1987.

In a brief text and in striking black-and-white photos, readers are given a close-up look into the lives of typical Amish children of today.

Galdone, Paul. ***The Monkey and the Crocodile.*** Clarion, 1969.

An adaptation from an East Indian fable.

Goble, Paul, and Dorothy Goble. ***The Friendly Wolf.*** Bradbury, 1974.

Little Cloud and Bright Eyes are plains Indians who get lost in the hills. A wolf befriends them, and wolves have been Indians' friends ever since.

Gray, Nigel. ***A Country Far Away.*** Orchard Books, 1989.

In this book, two parallel panels of illustrations depict the same daily events in two locations, one an African setting, the other a Western setting. This format points out similarities and differences.

Greenfield, Eloise. ***Under the Sunday Tree.*** Harper, 1989.

Ten poems reflecting Bahaman life are accompanied in this book by paintings by Amos Ferguson.

Grifalconi, Ann. ***The Village of Round and Square Houses.*** Little, Brown, 1986.

"Each one has a place apart, and a time to be together" in the village of Tas in the Cameroons. The men live in the square houses, and the women and the children live in the round houses. The origins of the custom provide a delightful story-within-the-story.

Grimm, Jacob, and Wilhelm Grimm. ***The Frog King and Other Tales of the Brothers Grimm.*** New American Library (Signet Classic), 1989.

This is a paperback collection of folktales for reading aloud.

Hansel and Gretel. Retold by Rika Lesser, pictures by Paul Zelinsky. Putnam, 1989.

The classic Grimm tale of courage in the face of frightening obstacles is retold in this book.

Heide, Florence Parry. ***The Day of Ahmed's Secret.*** Lothrop, 1990.

Contemporary life in the Eastern world provides a background for Ahmed's special secret: He has learned to read and write. The book is distinguished by its illustrations and engaging story. Students can identify with Ahmed while observing the differences between his outward world and theirs.

Her Seven Brothers. Illustrated by Paul Goble. Bradbury, 1988.

The author retells the Cheyenne legend in which a girl and her seven chosen brothers become the Big Dipper. See also *Iktomi and the Boulder: A Plains Indian Story* (Orchard Books, 1988).

Johnston, Tony. ***Pages of Music.*** Putnam, 1988.

Johnston's narrative and Tomie DePaola's illustrations tell a story of gratitude and love. The tale is set against a background that depicts life in rural Italy.

The Juniper Tree and Other Tales from Grimm.
Retold by Lore Segal. Farrar, 1973.

This is a teacher's resource of the Grimm's tales for telling or reading aloud. Appropriate at more than one grade level, it should be used discriminately.

Keats, Ezra Jack. *John Henry: An American Legend.* Knopf, 1967.

This is the retelling of an American folktale and the story of the men who laid the track for the iron horse that tied this nation together.

Lewis, Naomi. *The Twelve Dancing Princesses and Other Tales from Grimm.* Dial, 1986.

The 14 stories assembled here include such favorites as "Snow White," "Hansel and Gretel," and "Cinderella" along with lesser-known tales. The collection displays the full range of the Grimm brothers' talents.

Lewis, Patrick J. *The Tsar and the Amazing Cow.* Dial, 1988.

Buryonka, the faithful cow of an old Russian peasant couple, suddenly gives magic milk which brings youth and happiness to the couple but disaster to the wicked, greedy Tsar, who demands that the cow be brought to his grand palace in St. Petersburg.

McDermott, Gerald. *Anansi the Spider: A Tale from the Ashanti.* Holt, 1972.

In this African folktale, Anansi, a spider, is saved from terrible fates by his six sons and is unable to decide which of them to reward.

Martin, Bill, Jr., and John Archambault. *Knots on a Counting Rope.* Holt, 1987.

This is a poetic account, conveyed through dialogue, of the special bond between a blind Indian boy and his grandfather. The empathy and common memory of the two are strong. This book is usable also in other grades.

Once Upon a Time: A Book of Old-Time Fairy Tales. Edited by Katharine Bates. Rand McNally, reprint of 1921 original.

Most of the best-known, best-loved, traditional fairy tales are here, edited by the poet who authored "America, the Beautiful." The introduction points up the moral and spiritual values inherent in the tales.

The treasury is best suited for reading aloud, and most of Margaret Evans Price's illustrations are large enough for classroom viewing.

Peretz, I. L., and Uri Shulevitz. *The Magician.* Macmillan, 1985.

This is an unforgettable story for use at the Jewish holiday of Passover.

Phelps, Ethel J. *Tatterhood and Other Tales.* Feminist Press, 1978.

Authentic fairy tales with strong female protagonists are presented in this book. The stories are best suited for reading aloud or telling at this level.

Polacco, Patricia. *Rechenka's Eggs.* Philomel, 1988.

Babushka's beautiful, painted eggs always win first prize at the Easter festival. The festivals of old Moscow come to life in this beautiful folktale. See also *Uncle Vova's Tree* (1989).

Politi, Leo. *The Nicest Gift.* Scribner, 1973.

This gentle story set in East Los Angeles introduces Carlitos and his dog Blanco. Although the story is set at Christmastime, it can be shared anytime of the year. See also *Lito and the Clown* and *Moy Moy,* both now out of print but available in libraries.

Price, Margaret Evans. *A Child's Book of Myths and Enchantment Tales.* Checkerboard Press, 1989.

Traditional myths of Greece are retold here so that young children can understand them. Suggested for reading aloud, the tellings are untrammeled by genealogies or extraneous detail. In reprinting the book, the publisher faithfully preserved the art deco illustrations of the 70-year-old original.

Rodanus, Kristana. *The Story of Wali Dad.* Lothrop, 1988.

Wali Dad's selfless acts complicate the simple life he struggles to maintain in this lavishly illustrated tale from India.

Roland, Donna. *More of Grandfather's Stories from Cambodia.* Open My World Publishing Co., 1984.

Other volumes of folktales by this author include tales from Germany, Mexico, Vietnam, and the Philippines.

Say, Allen. ***The Bicycle Man.*** Parnassus Press, 1982.

Shortly after the end of World War II, the Japanese and American cultures happen "to meet" in a playground. The result is innocent and charming.

Shute, Linda. ***Momotaro, the Peach Boy.*** Lothrop, 1986.

In ancient Japanese belief, a peach had the power to bring happiness to the one who possessed it. This fable depicts Peach Boy's courage through acts of kindness. Source notes at the back of the book provide a pronunciation guide and helpful background information.

Steptoe, John. ***Mufaro's Beautiful Daughters: An African Tale.*** Lothrop, 1987.

Steptoe's lavish illustrations, expressive and detailed, distinguish this African folktale about the fate of two sisters, one kind, the other selfish.

Stevenson, James. ***When I Was Nine.*** Greenwillow, 1986.

This story describes a childhood summer in 1930 and provides a delightful way of telling children about the time when adults were children. Journal-keeping and autobiographical writing activities are introduced in this book.

Surat, Michele Maria. ***Angel Child, Dragon Child.*** Raintree, 1983.

Ut, a Vietnamese girl attending school in the United States, lonely for her mother left behind in Vietnam, makes a new friend who presents her with a wonderful gift.

Tales of the Wise and Foolish. Edited by Anne Rose Souby. Steck-Vaughn, 1990.

This paperbound book contains several folktales from around the world that allow students to consider the consequences of behavior. It is one of several volumes in Steck-Vaughn's FOLK TALES FROM AROUND THE WORLD series. Most of the tales are short and are recommended for reading aloud.

Tales from Grimm. Retold by Wanda Gag. Coward, 1981.

This collection and its companion, *More Tales from Grimm* (1974), are good sources of stories for reading aloud.

Tolstoy, Leo. ***Shoemaker Martin.*** Adapted by Brigette Hanhart. North-South Books (Holt), 1986.

Used in conjunction with other tales, this story helps to show similarities in world religions.

A Treasury of Turkish Folktales. Retold by Barbara Walker. Linnet Books, 1988.

Some of the shorter tales in this book (e.g., "The Lion's Den") lend themselves to storytelling at this grade level. The collection is exemplary for its authenticity and faithfulness to the originals. A pronunciation guide is included.

The Twelve Days of Christmas. Illustrated by Jan Brett. Putnam, 1986.

Each full-color two-page spread in this book reflects a different culture. The illustrations are truly breathtaking. See also *The Mitten* (Putnam, 1989).

Uchida, Yoshiko. ***Magic Listening Cap: More Folktales from Japan.*** Creative Arts Books, 1987.

These 14 short traditional tales, perfect for the storyteller, express a universality of characters and situations.

The Value of Friends. Illustrated by Eric Meller. Dharma Publishing Co., 1986.

Unusual illustrations accompany this tale from the Buddhist Jataka tales.

Williams, Jay. ***Everyone Knows What a Dragon Looks Like.*** Macmillan, 1976.

Though not a religious tale, this story contains an element of Taoist principles.

Yarborough, Camille. ***Cornrows.*** Coward, 1979.

This story is braided with love as Great Grandma puts cornrows (braids) into Mama's, Sister's, and Brother MeToo's hair. It is also the story of the origin in Africa of this hair-styling technique. It is a narrative about the power of love to enable one to rise above hardship and fill the family with a spirit of pride.

Yashima, Taro. ***Umbrella.*** Viking, 1958.

Exquisite pictures, finely illustrated endpapers, and a gentle, sweet story surrounding a little girl's birthday present are features of this book. See also *Crow Boy* (Viking, 1955).

Zalben, Jane. ***Beni's First Chanukah.*** Holt, 1988.

This is the story of Beni the bear's holiday celebration.

Grade Two:
People Who
Make a Difference

2.1 People Who Supply Our Needs

Aliki. *Corn Is Maize: The Gift of the Indians*. Harper, 1976.

In this book, we learn how Indian farmers thousands of years ago found and nourished a wild grass plant and made it an important part of their lives; how they learned the best ways to grow, store, and use its fat yellow kernels; and how they shared this knowledge with the new settlers of America.

Ancona, George. *Bananas from Manolo to Margie*. Clarion, 1982.

Ancona's book is illustrated with black-and-white photos. Though somewhat "text heavy" for second grade, its pictures and narration may be excerpted in order to help students better understand the geographical ramifications of food.

Barton, Byron. *Trucks*. Crowell, 1986.

This book joins Barton's *Trains* and *Boats* in depicting how goods are transported.

Dupasquier, Philippe. *Colección "Aquí Se Trabaja."* Madrid: Generales Anaya, 1985.

Titles: "El Aeropuerto" (The airport)
"El Garaje" (The garage)
"El Puerto" (The harbor)
"La Estación del Ferrocarril" (The railroad station)
"La Fábrica" (The factory)
"La Obra" (The construction)

These Spanish-language books explain how airports, train stations, harbors, and other places operate and how they depend on cooperation.

El Mercado. México: Editorial Patria (Colección Piñata), 1985.

This study of the marketplace and the array of people and wares to be found there is written in Spanish.

Gibbons, Gail. *The Milk Makers*. Macmillan, 1985.

This behind-the-scenes look at the dairy industry complements this unit. See also *Deadline! From News to Newspaper* (Crowell, 1987) and *Marge's Diner* by the same author.

Higgins, Susan Olson. *The Thanksgiving Book*. Pumpkin Press Publishing House, 1984.

This book is valuable as a teacher's resource. Despite some insignificant material, several items help address the framework in its emphasis on foods, poems, and facts regarding the first Thanksgiving.

Horwitz, Joshua. *Night Markets: Bringing Food to a City*. Crowell, 1984.

The problem of how to feed the huge population of New York City is detailed here in text and photographs. The wholesale markets that supply produce, meat, dairy products, flowers, and bakery goods are shown during the nighttime hours.

Jaspersohn, William. *Ice Cream*. Macmillan, 1988.

Economics, technology, and geography come together in making and distributing this "high interest" product.

Joly, Dominique. *Grains of Salt*. Charlesbridge Publishing, 1988.

The *YOUNG DISCOVERY* series contains other books dealing with metals, oil, wood, and so on. These books are small and are best suited for individual reading.

Kellogg, Steven. *Johnny Appleseed*. Morrow, 1988.

John Chapman sets out to plant apple trees in the American wilderness and becomes one of America's legendary heroes.

Kimmelman, Leslie. *Frannie's Fruits*. Harper, 1989.

The operation and business of a family-owned fruit stand are charmingly depicted here.

Lasky, Kathryn. *Sugaring Time*. Macmillan, 1983.

Black-and-white photographs illustrate this nonfiction work that well demonstrates the link between food and geography.

Lelord, Bijou. *Joseph and Nellie*. Bradbury, 1986.

This simple story recounts a day in the life of a

fishing family and delineates the responsibilities of each spouse.

McGovern, Ann. *The Pilgrims' First Thanksgiving.* Scholastic, 1988.

This paperback presents the traditional story of the Pilgrims in simple language.

Maestro, Betsy. *Ferryboat.* Crowell, 1986.

The daily and seasonal operation of a ferryboat is detailed in this first-person account of a crossing on the Chester-Hadlyme, Connecticut, ferry. A historical note and map are included.

Mitgutsch, Ali. *From Beet to Sugar.* Carolrhoda, 1981.

See also *From Blossom to Honey* (Carolrhoda, 1981). Mitgutsch has an extensive list of works that focus on foods, producers, and processes. Minón of Spain publishes Spanish-language versions of these books.

Patent, Dorothy Hinshaw. *Wheat: The Golden Harvest.* Putnam, 1987.

The excellent text and photographs in this book introduce our most important food—wheat—from its growth through harvest, to flour, and its use in pastas, breakfast cereals, and bread. This book can be used in conjunction with Ann Morris's *Bread, Bread, Bread* (Lothrop, 1989).

Perham, Molly. *People at Work.* Dillon, 1986.

The text and photographs in this book describe various jobs performed by people around the world, including nursing, fishing, sheep farming, filmmaking, and fire fighting.

Rickard, Graham. *Airports.* Bookwright, 1987.

This is an explanatory book with photographs. See also *Helicopters* by the same author.

Rogow, Zack. *Oranges.* Pictures by Mary Szilagyi. Orchard Books, 1988.

A good presentation of the geographic and economic aspects of fruit is included in this book.

Urrutia, Cristina. *El Maíz.* México: Libros del Rincón, SEP (Colección Chipichipi), 1989. Also, Editorial Patria (Colección Piñata, 1981).

This book points out the importance of corn and

complements this unit on producers, processors, and transporters of food. It is written in Spanish.

Ziefert, Harriet. *A New Coat for Anna.* Knopf, 1988.

Anna visits the sheep that provide wool, meets the woman who spins yarn, helps her mother dye yarn, brings yarn to the weaver, and goes to the tailor who makes her new winter coat in this book about barter and ingenuity after World War II.

2.2 Our Parents, Grandparents, and Ancestors from Long Ago

Aardema, Verna. *Rabbit Makes a Monkey of Lion.* Dial, 1989.

Jerry Pinkney's illustrations give visualization to a funny and perceptive story of the rabbit who likes honey.

Adler, David A. *A Picture Book of Passover.* Holiday, 1982.

Use this book in conjunction with Barbara Cohen's *The Carp in the Bathtub* (Kar-Ben Copies, Inc., 1987).

Aliki. *A Medieval Feast.* Crowell, 1983.

Brilliant colors and detailed drawings in this book bring to life the exotic feast that a medieval lord created for the king and his company, offering the reader an understanding of how people worked, looked, and thought centuries ago.

Anderson, Joy. *Juma and The Magic Jinn.* Lothrop, 1986.

Muslim Africa provides the setting and motifs for the tale of a boy whose three wishes show him that there is more magic at home than can be conjured from the family jinn jar.

Asbjornsen, P. C., and Jorgen Moe. *Norwegian Folk Tales.* Pantheon, 1982.

Selections from this book are suitable for both telling and reading aloud. Asbjornsen and Moe were the Grimm brothers of Norwegian folklore.

Blaine, Marge. *The Terrible Thing That Happened at Our House.* Scholastic, 1983.

When both parents become employed outside the home, a crisis is resolved with humor and understanding.

Brown, Marcia. *Once a Mouse.* Scribner, 1961.
A tale from the Indian Hitopadesa.

Bryan, Ashley. *Beat the Story-Drum, Pum-Pum.* Atheneum, 1980.
Bryan offers retellings from the African Hausa and other traditions. The stories are best read aloud or told at this grade level.

Clifford, Eth. *The Remembering Box.* Houghton, 1985.
A special bond of pride and love exists between grandparents who come from the Old World and their American-born grandchildren. Life was too hard for the grandparents to enjoy their own children when they were small; but for the grandchild who will listen, these grandparents have reminiscences that form a treasury of stories. This book is good for reading aloud at this grade.

Coerr, Eleanor. *The Josefina Story Quilt.* Harper, 1986.
Josefina is Faith's pet hen and companion during the family's journey to California in a covered wagon during the 1850s. Faith sews a patchwork quilt to recall their adventures.

Cohen, Barbara. *Yussel's Prayer: A Yom Kippur Story.* Lothrop, 1981.
This moving story is centered around a Jewish holiday.

Colección Libros para Mirar. Madrid: Altea, n.d.
Titles: "Así Son los Abuelos Que Viven Cerca" (Grandparents who live nearby)
"Así Son los Abuelos que Viven Lejos" (Grandparents who live far away)
"Así Son Papá y Mamá" (Father and mother)
"Así Son los Tíos" (Uncles and aunts)
This set contains ten Spanish-language titles about family relationships.

Credle, Ellis. *Down, Down the Mountain.* Lodestar, 1934.

This charming story of Appalachian life, set in the not-so-long-ago, is real Americana and worthy of republication.

DePaola, Tomie. *Nana Upstairs and Nana Downstairs.* Putnam, 1973.
This is the story of a boy's relationships with his grandmother and great-grandmother. When the great-grandmother dies, she becomes Nana "upstairs."

Ehrlich, Amy. *The Story of Hanukkah.* Dial, 1989.
This illustrated, historical account of the Maccabees explains the origin of the Jewish holiday.

Fearotte, Phyllis. *The You and Me Heritage Tree: Children's Crafts from 21 American Traditions.* Workman, 1976.
This book contains step-by-step instructions for more than 100 craft projects that reflect 22 different ethnic traditions in the United States. The projects require easily available materials.

Flournoy, Valerie. *The Patchwork Quilt.* Dial, 1989.
African-American family life is reflected in this story of love, caring, and a quilting project that is shared by grandmother and grandchild.

Fox, Mem. *Wilfrid Gordon McDonald Partridge.* Kane Miller Books, 1985.
This is a humorous tale that encompasses memory, recollection, and family history.

Freedman, Russell. *Children of the Wild West.* Clarion, 1983.
This is a realistic look at the hardships and adventures of children, both immigrant and Native American, in the nineteenth-century American West. Although the text is too advanced for this grade, the photographs authenticate a wealth of information on schools, homes, work, and play. There is a brief mention of the roles played by black and Mexican children.

Friedman, Ina R. *How My Parents Learned to Eat.* Houghton, 1984.
A child tells of the happy resolution of a slight problem stemming from diverse cultures within the same family.

Friego, Margot, and others. ***Tortillitas para Mamá.*** Holt, 1981.

> Hispanic nursery rhymes, well illustrated and in two languages, compose this book.

Galbraith, Kathryn O. ***Laura Charlotte.*** Philomel, 1990.

> Told with warm sentiment, this book relates a mother's recollection of childhood. It demonstrates how a hand-me-down toy can maintain a contact with the past.

Gibbons, Gail. ***Easter.*** Holiday, 1989.

> This book can enhance discussions of how families celebrate different holidays. See also this author's books on Christmas and Thanksgiving.

Goffstein, M. B. ***Laughing Latkes.*** Farrar, 1980.

> This is a graceful, charming book about the Jewish holiday of Chanukah.

Gray, Genevieve. ***How Far, Felipe?*** Harper, 1978.

> The travels of Felipe and his family as they move from Mexico to California are described in this book. Filomena, Felipe's burro, is to be left behind, but Felipe hides her among some other animals making the trip. This is an account of the 1775 expedition by Colonel Juan deAnza.

Greaves, Margaret. ***Once There Were No Pandas.*** Dutton, 1988.

> A gentle, pathetic tale from China, depicting love and sacrifice, is told in this book.

Grifalconi, Ann. ***Osa's Pride.*** Little, Brown, 1990.

> Osa's story is one of self-discovery, moral truth, and familial love, told with glowing illustrations reflecting African village life. See also *Praise and the Butterfly* by the same author.

Heller, Linda. ***The Castle of Hester Street.*** Jewish Publications Society, 1982.

> This picture book presents two views of the past. Julie's grandmother and grandfather together give her a complete picture of their past.

Hendershot, Judith. ***In Coal Country.*** Knopf, 1987.

> This story takes us back to a coal-mining town in the 1930s as a little girl tells what it was like to grow up there.

Highwater, Jamake. ***Moonsong Lullaby.*** Lothrop, 1981.

> This is a volume of exquisite poetry from the pen of one of our outstanding American Indian writers.

Johnston, Tony. ***The Quilt Story.*** Putnam, 1985.

> This book traces the story of a quilt, lovingly made by a pioneer mother. The quilt travels over time and generations to another little girl who finds comfort in its beauty. See also *Yonder* (Dial, 1988) by the same author.

Jukes, Mavis. ***Blackberries in the Dark.*** Knopf, 1985.

> Austin's beloved grandfather has died. In this gentle story, he and his grandmother come to terms with their loss and discover a new relationship with each other.

Lang, Andrew. *THE FAIRY BOOK* series. Amereon House or Dover Reprints, various dates.

> The books in this classic series by Lang are color-coded (e.g., *The Red Fairy Book, The Gray Fairy Book*) and encompass folktales from around the world. Lang's nineteenth-century prose style may not be appropriate for all classes; teachers should choose stories to read or tell. See also Ethel J. Phelps's *Tatterhood and Other Tales* (Feminist Press, 1978) in the entries for Grade 1.3.

Lawson, Robert. ***They Were Strong and Good.*** Viking, 1940.

> "This is the story of my mother and my father and of their fathers and mothers," the author writes. Portions of this book may be excerpted.

Lee, Jeanne. ***Toad Is the Uncle of Heaven.*** Holt, 1985.

> This Vietnamese folktale relates how Toad earned the respectful title of "uncle." See also *Ba-Nam* by the same author.

LeShan, Eda. ***Grandparents: A Special Kind of Love.*** Macmillan, 1984.

> Written with care and sensitivity, this book explores the unique relationship between grandchildren and grandparents. Advice for dealing with conflicts and problems between generations is simply stated.

Lin, Adet. ***The Milky Way and Other Chinese Folk Tales.*** Harcourt, 1961.

"How the Miser Turned into a Donkey," one of the tales in this book, is from the Taoist culture.

The Little Snowgirl: An Old Russian Tale. Adapted by Carolyn Croll. Putnam, 1989.

Childless parents experience the power of love when their snow child comes alive in this story. The Russian setting is appealing.

Locker, Thomas. ***Family Farm.*** Dial, 1988.

Members of a farm family nearly lose their home until they hit on the idea of growing and selling pumpkins and flowers to supplement their sales of corn and milk.

McCurdy, Michael. ***Hannah's Farm: Seasons on an Early American Homestead.*** Holiday, 1988.

Seasonal changes dictate daily activities on a nine-teenth-century farm in the Berkshire hills of Massachusetts.

Mikolaycak, Charles. ***Babushka: An Old Russian Tale.*** Holiday, 1984.

Vivid colors and intricate patterns of cloth and costume are richly illustrated in this eastern European Christmas tale of the wondering Babushka. See also Mikolaycak's version of *The Christmas Story.*

Mwalimu. ***Awful Aardvark.*** Little, Brown, 1982.

Why do aardvarks sleep all day? The answer is contained in this authentic African tale.

One Little Goat: A Passover Song. Edited by Marilyn Hirsh. Holiday, 1979.

This Jewish folksong is sung at Passover. The musical score is included along with brief information about Passover and the song.

Parramón, J. M., María Rius, and Carmen Sole Vendrell. ***Colección las Cuatro Edades.*** Barcelona: Parramón Ediciones, 1985. (U.S.: Barron's.)

Titles: "Los Niños" (Children)
 "Los Jóvenes" (Teenagers, youth)
 "Los Padres" (Parents)
 "Los Abuelos" (Grandparents)

Matching English versions of these Spanish editions depicting the "four ages" of human existence are available.

Polacco, Patricia. ***The Keeping Quilt.*** Simon and Schuster, 1988.

Family heritage and history are reflected in the quilt that enfolds the new infant.

Politi, Leo. ***Three Stalks of Corn.*** Macmillan, 1976.

This book features tall legends of how corn came to be used in Mexico and of the relationship between the serpent god Quetzalcoatl and corn. The legends add dimension to a story of a grandmother and her wonderful cooking.

Pomerantz, Charlotte. ***The Chalk Doll.*** Lippincott, 1989.

Stories of a Jamaican childhood are shared between a mother and daughter in this illustrated book that depicts a Caribbean culture.

A Precious Life. Illustrated by Rosalyn White. Dharma Publishing Co., 1989.

The Jataka tales are similar in structure to fables and reflect Buddhist teachings and beliefs.

Quayle, Eric. ***The Shining Princess and Other Japanese Legends.*** Arcade, 1989.

Ten Japanese folktales contained herein provide examples of the humor and wisdom to be found in folklore. The tellings are best read aloud at this grade level.

Red Hawk, Richard. ***Grandmother's Christmas Story: A True Tale of the Quechan Indians.*** Sierra Oaks, 1988.

This author specializes in authentic Indian tales, including Navajo and Hopi stories.

Reyher, Becky. ***My Mother Is the Most Beautiful Woman in the World.*** Lothrop, 1945.

An endearing folktale of familial love set in a Russian village is this book's subject.

Rogers, Paul. ***From Me to You.*** Orchard, 1988.

A story of recollection showing how artifacts or hand-me-downs reveal family history.

Silent Night. Illustrated by Susan Jeffers. Dutton, 1984.

This world-famous Austrian carol has crossed into many cultures and languages.

Simoes Coelho, Ronaldo. *Macaquino*. México: Libros del Rincón, SEP (Colección Chipichipi), 1988.

Paternal love within a family is the focus of this story. It is written in Spanish.

Smucker, Anna Egan. *No Star Nights*. Knopf, 1989.

Childhood memories of Weirton, West Virginia, provide the basis for this memoir of life in a steel-mill town. Students can look for ways in which an industry can form a town's way of life. The concluding page points up the inevitability of change.

Sonneborn, Ruth. *Friday Night Is Papa Night*. Penguin, 1970.

Papa works away from home and is able to return only on weekends, which makes Friday night all the more special.

Steptoe, John. *The Story of Jumping Mouse*. Lothrop, 1984.

This is an American Indian story of haunting beauty. The late John Steptoe was a leading writer-illustrator.

Stolz, Mary. *Storm in the Night*. Harper, 1988.

Grandfather tells Thomas a tale of when he was a boy. Beautiful use of language in this book conveys the warm relationship between grandfather and grandson.

Suyeoka, George. *Issun Boshi*. Honolulu: Island Heritage, 1974.

This story is based on the famous "Inch Boy" legend, which predates Buddhism.

Tadjo, Veronique. *Lord of the Dance: An African Retelling*. Lippincott, 1989.

Poetry and Senufo-style art are employed to recount this story from the Ivory Coast. The mask, Lord of the Dance, is worn during ceremonial dances.

Townsend, Maryann. *Pop's Secret*. Addison-Wesley, 1980.

In this story, a young boy relates his experiences with his grandfather. Family album photographs show the advances from infancy to old age and the thread of inheritance woven into a family. Pop, the grandfather, dies, and the family continues on—sadder for the loss but richer for the love.

Turner, Ann. *Dakota Dugout*. Macmillan, 1985.

A vigorous woman describes her experiences as a young bride living in a sod house on the Dakota prairie. Oral family history is a powerful means of imparting a common memory.

Uchida, Yoshiko. *The Dancing Kettle*. Creative Arts Books, 1986.

This collection of myths and legends of Japan contains stories that relate to Shinto principles.

Weitzman, David. *My Backyard History Book*. Little, Brown, 1975.

This book provides a practical, motivating introduction to historic events. It is useful for teachers as well as students.

Wilder, Laura Ingalls. *LITTLE HOUSE* series. Harper, various dates.

The family unit is beautifully reflected in this series. Selected chapters from Wilder's *Farmer Boy* are especially enjoyed at this level (e.g., "Surprise") and are recommended for reading aloud.

Williams, Vera B. *A Chair for My Mother*. Greenwillow, 1984.

The story of a young girl and her mother, who save money to buy an easy chair following a fire in their apartment, is told in this loving portrait of a single-parent household.

Williams, Vera B. *Stringbean's Trip to the Shining Sea*. Greenwillow, 1988.

In this book, postcards provide a history of a cross-country journey. Students can research locales, create maps, and write postcards recording a fictional family's trip to California.

Wisniewski, David. *The Warrior and the Wise Man*. Lothrop, 1989.

The Emperor of Japan tells his sons that his successor shall be the one who brings him the five eternal elements. The tale stems from ancient Japanese culture.

Yashima, Taro. *Crow Boy*. Viking, 1955.

This well-known story, set in Japan, is about prejudice and appreciation of others.

Yolen, Jane. *Favorite Folktales from Around the World.* Pantheon Books, 1986.

This collection is a sizable resource containing stories for telling or reading aloud. It is also usable at other grade levels.

2.3   People from Many Cultures, Now and Long Ago

Adler, David A. *A Picture Book of Martin Luther King, Jr.* Holiday, 1989.

Strengthened throughout his childhood to withstand prejudice by the love of his parents, King turned as a young man to the ministry as a means to help his people regain pride and their civil rights. See also *Picture Book of Benjamin Franklin, Picture Book of Thomas Jefferson,* and *Thomas Alva Edison: Great Inventor* (Holiday, 1990) by the same author.

Aliki. *A Weed Is a Flower: The Life of George Washington Carver.* Simon and Schuster, 1988.

This book is a reverent, loving depiction of George Washington Carver's life and achievements. See also Aliki's *The Story of William Penn* (Prentice-Hall, 1964) and *The Many Lives of Benjamin Franklin* (Simon and Schuster, 1988).

Behrens, June. *Sally Ride, Astronaut: An American First.* Children's Press, 1984.

Ride is not only the first American woman to orbit the earth but is also the youngest American astronaut to do so. Her colorful career interests many youngsters. The book is more useful for its pictures and information than for its narrative quality.

Brighton, Catherine. *Five Secrets in a Box.* Dutton, 1987.

Galileo's daughter, Virginia, opens a gold box only to discover her famous father's instruments, and they reveal the world to her in a new and wonderful way.

Collins, David R. *The Country Artist: A Story About Beatrix Potter.* Carolrhoda, 1988.

This book can be read aloud in conjunction with Potter's own pictures and stories. Potter made a difference through the beauty she brought to young lives. She was a "Miss Rumphius" of her time and place.

Davidson, Margaret. *Louis Braille: The Boy Who Invented Books for the Blind.* Scholastic, 1974.

An inspiring life for youngsters to know and understand is described in this book.

Ferris, Jeri. *What Do You Mean? A Story About Noah Webster.* Carolrhoda, 1988.

This is the story of Noah Webster and his impact on the English-speaking world. See also Ferris's book on Benjamin Banneker, *What Are You Figuring Now?*

Fritz, Jean. *And Then What Happened, Paul Revere?* Coward, 1973.

This good-humored, unconventional recounting of Paul Revere's life and times succeeds in humanizing the man behind the legend. Numerous Fritz titles are available, and all are usable.

Gerrard, Roy. *Sir Francis Drake and His Daring Deeds.* Farrar, 1988.

The adventures and accomplishments of this "lion-hearted little chap" are related through picture and verse and are told with humor in this book.

Greenfield, Eloise. *Rosa Parks.* Crowell, 1973.

The inspiring story of a simple act that changed history is told in this book.

Johnson, Spencer. *The Value of Believing in Yourself: The Story of Louis Pasteur.* Value Communications, 1976.

This tale about Louis Pasteur is based on events in his life. Some historical facts are included.

Kent, Zachary. *The Story of Clara Barton.* Children's Press, 1987.

The founder of the American Red Cross deserves new attention as the United States faces a nursing shortage in the 1990s.

Lepthien, Emilie U. *Corazon Aquino, President of the Philippines.* Children's Press, 1987.

Though Aquino's life was marred by violent tragedy, her quiet courage and determination have been key elements in overcoming hardships. Parts of her biography require careful forethought for presentation at this grade level.

Lobel, Arnold. ***On the Day Peter Stuyvesant Sailed into Town.*** Harper, 1971.

Despite his intimidating personality, Stuyvesant saw New Amsterdam through difficult times—and a community renewal project. His story is told in verse.

Mitchell, Barbara. ***Shoes for Everyone: A Story About Jan Matzeliger.*** Carolrhoda, 1986.

This is an inspiring, little-known story of oppression, creativity, and American heritage. See also this author's *America, I Hear You: A Story About George Gershwin* (Carolrhoda, 1987) and *Raggin' : A Story About Scott Joplin* (Carolrhoda, 1987).

Monjo, F. N. ***The One Bad Thing About Father.*** Harper, 1970.

This is a biography of Theodore Roosevelt, one of the most extraordinary men to occupy the White House, as it might have been told by Roosevelt's son, Quentin.

Provensen, Alice, and Martin Provensen. ***The Glorious Flight: Across the Channel with Louis Bleriot.*** Viking, 1987.

This is a biography of the man whose fascination with flying machines produced the Bleriot XI, which crossed the English Channel in 37 minutes in the early 1900s.

Quackenbush, Robert. ***Along Came the Model T!*** Four Winds, 1978.

Henry Ford's obsession with building a smaller, lightweight, horseless carriage is traced in this book from his childhood delight in fixing watches and repairing toys through his early experimentation to his success with the Model T. A diagram of how a car works is included.

Roberts, Naurice. ***Henry Cisneros.*** Children's Press, 1988.

These picture-story biographies feature black-and-white photos with sparse, factual information. The example of the noted San Antonio mayor can encourage students toward civic participation and involvement.

Roop, Peter, and Connie Roop. ***Keep the Lights Burning, Abbie.*** Carolrhoda, 1985.

In 1856, a storm delays the lighthouse keeper's return to an island off the coast of Maine, and his daughter must keep the lights burning herself. This true story demonstrates steadfastness and courage.

Sabin, Louis. ***Marie Curie.*** Troll, 1985.

Specializing in paperbacks, Troll produces a number of biographies that are inexpensive and accessible. Jackie Robinson, Elizabeth Blackwell, Jim Thorpe, and others are subjects.

Stanley, Diane. ***Peter the Great.*** Macmillan, 1986.

This is a biography of the czar who began the transformation of Russia into a modern state in the late seventeenth and early eighteenth centuries. The text is advanced for some second graders.

Turner, Glennette Tilley. ***Take a Walk in Their Shoes.*** Cobblehill Books, 1989.

Although the language and format of this book are better suited to somewhat older students, teachers may use the short play about Charles Drew as a content-appropriate teaching strategy in studying biographies.

Grade Three:
Continuity and Change

3.1 Our Local History: Discovering Our Past and Our Traditions

Some explanation is necessary regarding the books that are listed for this unit.

School districts will need to rely on sources in their own vicinities to amass stories, legends, and background data that relate to community and regional histories. Sources can include public libraries, historical societies, museums' bookstores, and local writers' organizations. The offices of some state landmarks maintain gift shops that stock pertinent materials, and many bookstores have sections devoted to books of local and regional interest.

Consequently, the titles listed here under "Our Local History" focus on generic rather than community-specific historical and geographic materials and emphasize the concept of change and continuity.

Burton, Virginia Lee. *The Little House.* Houghton, 1978.

A little house built in the country experiences many changes as the city grows up around it.

Carey, Helen, and Deborah R. Hanka. *How to Use Your Community as a Resource.* Watts, 1983.

Although intended for older students, this book offers teachers some helpful suggestions for researching and presenting local history.

Cartwright, Sally. *What's in a Map?* Putnam, 1976.

This book begins by asking children to think about their own life space, their world, and their relationship to it. They are shown how to map that world by using blocks, paper and pencil, and their imaginations.

Chambers, Catherine E. *Frontier Village: A Town Is Born.* Troll, 1984.

In this book, the reader follows the establishment of a tiny frontier town in Wisconsin over a four-year period.

Gibbons, Gail. *From Pathway to Highway: The Story of the Boston Post Road.* Harper, 1986.

The road, today a much-traveled four-lane highway, was once a path used by native Americans who traveled the eastern woodlands. In later years, the path was expanded and fortified by settlers who traveled from New York to Boston.

Goodall, John S. *The Story of an English Village.* Atheneum, 1979.

The growth of an English village from medieval times to the present, as seen from the same viewpoint every hundred years, is traced in this book. It is a good example of community change and continuity.

Lent, Blair. *Bayberry Bluff.* Houghton, 1987.

This is the story of an island that evolves from a summer tenting ground to a village of brightly painted and decorated houses.

Levinson, Riki. *I Go with My Family to Grandma's.* Dutton, 1986.

At the turn of the century, five little cousins from New York City accompany their families to Grandma's. Illustrations of clothing, furniture, modes of transportation, and the life-styles of the period are included in this book.

Müller, Jorg. *The Changing City.* Atheneum, 1977.

This portfolio consists of eight full-color foldout pictures showing the changing city. See also *The Changing Countryside* by the same author.

Parnall, Peter. *The Mountain.* Doubleday, 1971.

Change, continuity, geography, and ecology come together in a picture book that "bites." This book deserves republication.

Politi, Leo. *Little Leo.* Scribners, 1951.

Though dated, this book cleverly shows how one culture can influence individuals and other cultures. The characteristics of various settings are noteworthy for certain geographical themes. This book is worthy of republication.

Precek, Katharine Wilson. *Penny in the Road.* Macmillan, 1989.

A grandfather's recollections of finding an early American coin reflect change and continuity in our nation's ways of life. This book will help round out the third grade study of these themes.

Pryor, Bonnie. *House on Maple Street.* Morrow, 1987.

During the course of 300 years, many people have passed by or lived on the spot now occupied by a house numbered 107 Maple Street.

Turner, Ann. *Heron Street.* Harper, 1989.

This book ties together change, continuity, and American history and is a good book with which to conclude the school year.

Von Tscharner, Renata, and Ronald Fleming. *New Providence: A Changing Cityscape.* Harcourt, 1987.

The text and illustrations in this book trace the evolution of an imaginary but typical American city from the turn of the century to the 1980s.

Wheatley, Nadia, and Donna Rawlins. *My Place.* Australia in Print, 1989.

Change and continuity are depicted in an Australian community, beginning in the late 1980s and moving back to 1788. Each stop in time is marked by the recollections of fictional characters. The conclusion has a gentle, ironic twist.

Wynne, Annette. "Indian Children," in *Sung Under the Silver Umbrella.* Macmillan, 1935.

An old favorite, this poem expresses awe and wonder at the changes reflected in one community. It is also found in other anthologies such as *The Sound of Poetry, Gaily We Parade,* and *Time for Poetry.*

Zolotow, Charlotte. *The Sky Was Blue.* Harper, 1963.

A mother and daughter's conversation, as recounted in this book, encompasses both ephemeral and enduring aspects of life.

3.2 Our Nation's History: Meeting People, Ordinary and Extraordinary, Through Biography, Story, Folktale, and Legend

Adler, David A. *Thomas Jefferson: Father of Our Democracy.* Holiday, 1987.

This book presents a portrait of one of the truly important men in American history. It includes Jefferson's positions on issues of his day. See also *Washington, Father of Our Country.*

Alexander, Sue. *America's Own Holidays: Días de Fiesta de los Estados Unidos.* Watts, 1988.

Sandra Martín Arnold's Spanish translation of this book parallels Alexander's English-language original. This book is ideal for bilingual classrooms because of its discussion of national holidays.

Anno, Mitsumasa. *Anno's U.S.A.* Putnam, 1988.

Come along with world-famous artist Mitsumasa Anno for a wonder-filled exploration of the United States, its fabulous cities, and its inhabitants at work and at play. Seen through the eyes of this imaginative artist are the landscape, folklore, history, and traditions of our heritage.

Behrens, June. *Miss Liberty: First Lady of the World.* Children's Press, 1986.

Color photos and other visual elements illustrate this easy-to-read book.

Benchley, Nathaniel. *George, the Drummer Boy.* Harper, 1977.

When word reaches General Gage that the Minutemen are hiding cannons and gunpowder in Concord, Massachusetts, George, a British drummer boy, goes with the soldiers to capture it. This book is easy reading for third-grade students. See also *Sam, the Minuteman* by the same author.

Benet, Rosemary, and Stephen Vincent Benet. *A Book of Americans.* Holt, 1987.

Students will easily enjoy a number of these good-natured poems about the personalities and accomplishments of notable Americans. This book is also usable at the fifth-grade level.

Bierhorst, John. *Doctor Coyote: A Native American Aesop's Fables.* Illustrated by Wendy Watson. Macmillan, 1987.

This book contains 20 less-than-a-page-long fables whose passage from Aesop to Aztec to New Mexico has been researched by a noted folklorist. It is illustrated and humorous.

Brenner, Barbara. *Wagon Wheels.* Harper, 1978.

Three boys and their father travel from Kentucky to

Kansas. Their mother dies on the way, and the four of them have to make a home. The Kansas winter is unusually hard—and then the Indians come. This book is based on the true story of an adventurous African-American family.

Bulla, Clyde Robert. *Squanto, Friend of the Pilgrims.* Scholastic, 1988.

This is the biography of the man who taught the Europeans who came to the New World how to live and flourish.

Bunting, Eve. *The Wall.* Clarion, 1990.

A young boy and his father visit the Vietnam Veterans Memorial in this moving, low-key picture book. Bunting's *How Many Days to America? A Thanksgiving Story* (Clarion, 1988) is also recommended.

Chase, Richard. *The Jack Tales.* Houghton, 1943.

Chase is an authority on southern and Appalachian folktales. His other collections, such as *Grandfather Tales,* provide teachers with excellent folk material from which to select.

Child, Lydia Maria. *Over the River and Through the Wood.* Illustrated by Brinton Turkle. Putnam, 1974.

This classic song, first published in 1844, is treasured by young and old alike.

Coerr, Eleanor. *Lady with a Torch.* Harper, 1986.

This illustrated story relates how the Statue of Liberty was created. The book contains appendixes with factual information.

Cohen, Barbara. *Molly's Pilgrim.* Illustrated by Michael Deraney. Lothrop, 1983.

A touching story of an immigrant child from Russia who teaches her classmates the real meaning of Thanksgiving is related in this book.

Cooney, Barbara. *Island Boy.* Viking, 1988.

This book traces New England's history, culture, societal changes, and family ties through four generations. It awakens feelings of pride in our American heritage.

Costabel, Eva Deutsch. *The Jews of New Amsterdam.* Atheneum, 1988.

The 23 Jews who arrived in New Amsterdam in 1654 caused apprehension in the Dutch, and later British, colony. This excellent account helps to balance the misconception that colonial America was a land of freedom and equality for all groups.

Cunningham, William. *The Story of Daniel Boone.* Scholastic, 1964.

This book retells the legends and life of Daniel Boone.

Dalgliesh, Alice. *The Courage of Sarah Noble.* Macmillan, 1987.

Eight-year-old Sarah, wrapped in a cloak and told to keep up her courage, is sent to the wilderness in 1707 to cook and care for her father. Her many adventures involve threatening wolves, unfriendly strangers, and Indians. This book is based on an actual incident. See also *The Thanksgiving Story* (Macmillan, 1985) by the same author.

D'Aulaire, Ingri, and Edgar P. Parin. *Columbus.* Doubleday, 1987.

Fine black-and-white and colored illustrations fill the pages of this excellent biography of the great adventurer. See also *Benjamin Franklin, George Washington,* and other biographies by the same authors.

De Angeli, Marguerite. *Yonie Wondernose.* Doubleday, 1989.

This long-awaited republication of a 1940s classic depicts the life of an Amish boy. See also *Thee, Hannah* by the same author.

de Kay, James T. *Meet Martin Luther King, Jr.* Random, 1969.

One of the biographies in the STEP UP series, de Kay's work is simple enough to be read independently by many third graders. Biographies of other notables are also available in this series and may be useful for some fifth graders as well.

DePaola, Tomie. *An Early American Christmas.* Holiday, 1987.

In the early 1800s, Christmas was not celebrated as elaborately as it is today. This is the story of a German family and its rich Christmas traditions from the old country. From making bayberry candles to cutting down the Christmas tree, the family joyously prepares for Christmas.

The Diane Goode Book of American Folk Tales and Songs. Illustrated by Diane Goode; collected by Ann Dorell. Dutton, 1989.

The ethnic representation in this illustrated collection helps address our national identity through folktales.

Dunbar, Paul Laurence. *Candle-Lightin' Time.* AMS Press, reprint of 1901 edition.

Many of Dunbar's poems are enjoyed by children, "Amanda Kneading Dough" among them. Dunbar's works should be a part of every child's cultural literacy.

Fearotte, Phyllis. *The You and Me Heritage Tree: Children's Crafts from 21 American Traditions.* Workman, 1976.

Step-by-step instructions are included in this book for more than 100 craft projects from 22 different ethnic traditions in the United States. Easily available materials are used in these projects.

Feeney, Stephanie. *A Is for Aloha.* University of Hawaii Press, 1985.

Good photographs in this book help to reflect the variety and richness of our nation's culture.

Ferris, Jeri. *Go Free or Die: A Story About Harriet Tubman.* Carolrhoda, 1988.

A courageous woman, born a slave, Harriet Tubman escaped and over the next ten years returned the South to lead over 300 people out of slavery. She served as a scout, cook, and spy for the Union army and fought for human rights. See also *Walking the Road to Freedom: A Story About Sojourner Truth* by the same author.

Fisher, Leonard Everett. *The Statue of Liberty.* Holiday, 1985.

This book recounts the history of one of the largest monuments in the world, including how it was executed in France, shipped to America, and erected in New York harbor. See also *The White House* (Holiday, 1989) by the same author.

Fleming, Alice. *The King of Prussia and a Peanut Butter Sandwich.* Scribner, 1988.

This historical narrative traces the path of the Mennonites from Prussia to the Russian steppes and finally to the state of Kansas.

Fritz, Jean. *Will You Sign Here, John Hancock?* Coward, 1976.

This book provides an affectionate look at a flamboyant, egocentric, but kindly patriot and presents a most enjoyable view of history. See also *Can't You Make Them Behave, King George?* (Coward, 1982) and *George Washington's Breakfast* (Coward, 1984) by the same author.

Goble, Paul. *Buffalo Woman.* Bradbury, 1984.

This retelling of an Indian myth moves rapidly and conveys in vivid detail the theme "we are all related."

Good, Merle. *Nicole Visits an Amish Farm.* Walker, 1982.

Nicole, a child from the city, spends part of the summer on an Amish farm. Not only does she learn about Amish traditions but she also participates in some of the farm chores.

Greenfield, Eloise. *Mary McLeod Bethune.* Crowell, 1977.

This chronicle of the life of Mary McLeod Bethune begins with her childhood and continues until her death in 1955. The message she left was that children must never stop wanting to build a better world. See also Greenfield's book of poetry, *Honey, I Love: And Other Love Poems* (Harper, 1986).

Griffin, Judith Berry. *Phoebe the Spy.* Scholastic, 1977.

Originally published as *Phoebe and the General,* this paperback book tells of Phoebe Fraunces, the daughter of a tavern keeper, who spies for the cause of General George Washington. Griffin tells an exciting, true story.

Gross, Ruth Belov. *If You Grew Up with George Washington.* Scholastic, 1985.

The place and period in which our first President lived is deftly explored in question-and-answer form. The paperback *IF YOU* series is a useful addition at this grade level.

Haley, Gail. *Jack Jouett's Ride.* Viking, 1973.

In this book, the story is told of how Jack Jouett

warned Thomas Jefferson and the people of Charlottesville, Virginia, that the British were riding to capture the city and its revolutionary leaders.

Harvey, Brett. *Immigrant Girl: Becky of Eldridge Street.* Holiday, 1987.

Superb drawings combined with sensitive, fine writing make this story of Russian immigrants living in New York City in 1910 a valuable addition to our national identity. The book is based on the diary of a young girl.

Hodgson, Harriet. *My First Fourth of July Book.* Children's Press, 1987.

This is a collection of poems about traditional celebrations of America's independence. The poems describe picnics, fireworks, and bicycle parades.

Keithahn, Edward L. *Alaskan Igloo Tales.* Alaskan Northwest Books (GTE Discovery Publications), 1974.

This unique paperbound collection of authentic tales from an American Indian culture is often overlooked. See also *I Am Eskimo* from the same publisher.

Kellogg, Steven. *Pecos Bill.* Morrow, 1986.

Steven Kellogg has captured all the swirling vigor and energy of the frontier in this hilarious portrait of Pecos Bill, whose time and story are an essential part of our American heritage. See also *Paul Bunyan* (Morrow, 1988) by the same author.

Lawson, Robert. *Watchwords of Liberty: A Pageant of American Quotations.* Little, Brown, 1986.

Children should be familiar with a number of historic statements and shibboleths, and Lawson presents them in clear context and background. The segments in this book are short and can be shared over a period of days.

Lester, Julius. *The Tales of Uncle Remus: The Adventures of Brer Rabbit.* Dial, 1987.

Forty-eight Brer Rabbit tales are retold in modified, contemporary southern black English. Compare this book with Joel Chandler Harris's *The Complete Tales of Uncle Remus* (Houghton, 1955).

Levinson, Riki. *Watch the Stars Come Out.* Dutton, 1985.

The poignant story-within-a-story of immigration to the United States in the early 1890s is told in this book. The experience of the transatlantic crossing and the bewildering formalities associated with arriving in New York are seen from a child's perspective and deepen the young reader's understanding of this vital time in our history.

Lewis, Thomas P. *Clipper Ship.* Harper, 1978.

Captain Murdock is accompanied by his wife and children on the clipper ship *Rainbird* as she voyages from New York around Cape Horn to San Francisco. This easy-to-read book is based on fact, and the illustrations are appealing and well researched.

Livingston, Myra Cohn. *Celebrations.* Holiday, 1985.

This collection of poems deals with the holidays of the year. Apropos to this unit are poems about Martin Luther King Day, Labor Day, Thanksgiving, the Fourth of July, Memorial Day, and Presidents' Day.

Longfellow, Henry Wadsworth. *Hiawatha.* Illustrated by Susan Jeffers. Dial, 1983.

This is a beautifully illustrated version of the classic poem of an Indian boy's childhood learning about the stars and animals. See also Errol LeCain's version (Viking, 1976).

Lydon, Kerry Raines. *A Birthday for Blue.* Albert Whitman, 1989.

As his family travels west along the Cumberland Road, seven-year-old Blue celebrates his birthday in an unforgettable manner.

McGovern, Ann. *Secret Soldier: The Story of Deborah Sampson.* Scholastic, 1975.

This is the true story of an adventurous young girl who joined the army disguised as a boy during the American War of Independence.

Miller, Natalie. *The Story of the Lincoln Memorial.* Children's Press, 1966.

This book can be used in the third-grade study of our nation's shrines and symbols. One of the CORNERSTONES OF FREEDOM series, Miller's *Story of the Star-Spangled Banner* (1965) is also usable at the third-grade level.

Mitchell, Barbara. *A Pocketful of Goobers: A Story About George Washington Carver.* Carolrhoda, 1986.

This book relates the scientific efforts of George Washington Carver, especially his development of more than 300 uses for the peanut.

Monjo, F. N. *The Drinking Gourd.* Harper, 1969.

A quick-witted young boy helps an escaping slave family follow the drinking gourd (Big Dipper) along the Underground Railway to freedom. See also *King George's Head Was Made of Lead* and *Poor Richard in France* by the same author.

Munro, Roxie. *The Inside Outside Book of Washington, D.C.* Dutton, 1987.

The interior of 12 sites that capture the spirit of the nation's capital are rendered in detailed, full-color illustrations in this book. The landmarks are identified and information about each setting is included.

Nashone. *Grandmother Stories of the Northwest.* Sierra Oaks, 1988.

These authentic Indian tales are told by a kindly grandmother.

Politi, Leo. *Pedro, the Angel of Olvera Street.* Scribner, 1946.

This story is about the famous Las Posadas celebration on Olvera Street in Los Angeles and Pedro, a little boy, who played the part of an angel. See Politi's *Mieko* and *Mr. Fong's Toy Shop* for Asian-American stories. These books are out of print but may be available in libraries.

Prolman, Marilyn. *The Story of Mount Rushmore.* Children's Press, 1969.

This book can join others that depict our national shrines and symbols. See also Natalie Miller's *The Story of the Liberty Bell.*

Provensen, Alice. *Shaker Lane.* Grossman, 1987.

When the town decides to build a reservoir on their land, the residents of Shaker Lane decide to move away rather than fight to keep their homes.

Purdy, Carol. *Iva Dunnit and the Big Wind.* Dial, 1985.

Bold, broad drawings by Steven Kellogg illustrate this grand tale in the American tall-tale tradition. Iva Dunnit and her six children live alone on the prairie. One day a big wind comes up and Iva must use her wits to save her best laying hens and her house.

Quackenbush, Robert. *Old Silver Legs Takes Over: A Story of Peter Stuyvesant.* Prentice Hall, 1986.

The boisterous life of New Amsterdam's most colorful leader is described here. See also Quackenbush's *Watt Got You Started, Mr. Fulton?* (Prentice Hall, 1982), a story of James Watt and Robert Fulton; and *Pop! Goes the Weasel and Yankee Doodle: New York in 1776 and Today, with Songs and Pictures* (Harper, 1988).

Rappaport, Doreen. *Trouble at the Mines.* Crowell, 1987.

The 1899 Arnot, Pennsylvania, coal miners' strike is the basis for the plot of this personal narrative of Rosie Wilson, a daughter of a miner. Mary Harris, known as Mother Jones, provides assistance to the miners.

Ray, Deborah Kogan. *My Daddy Was a Soldier.* Holiday, 1990.

Personal history is told through the eyes of Jeanie, who recalls what her life was like in America during World War II.

Red Hawk, Richard. *A, B, C's The American Indian Way.* Sierra Oaks, 1988.

This book contains an alphabet that presents cultural features of American Indians. Photographs illustrate the prose.

Rice, James. *Texas Alphabet.* Pelican Publishing Co., 1988.

This book provides a lighthearted introduction to the Alamo, Sam Houston, Ponce de Leon, and a motley cast of jackrabbits, wolves, and oil wells.

Riley, James Whitcomb. "When the Frost Is on the Punkin," in *The Family Album of Favorite Poems.* Edited by P. Edward Ernest. Putnam, 1959.

This famous verse by Indiana's "Hoosier poet" is a part of U.S. cultural literacy and is often associated with Thanksgiving. Written so as to suggest Hoosier dialect, the poem is both tender and humorous in depicting rural pleasures of harvest time long ago. "Little Orphan Annie," "The Raggedy Man," and

"Out to Old Aunt Mary's" are other poems by Riley that reflect the same era and locale and that can be found in various anthologies.

Rollo, Vera. *The American Flag.* Maryland Historical Press, 1989.

This handy booklet contains concise, illustrated background material for the study of our national symbols in the third grade. It is a useful teacher's resource.

Roop, Peter, and Connie Roop. *Buttons for General Washington.* Carolrhoda, 1986.

In the fall of 1777, fourteen-year-old John Darragh takes coded messages his mother sewed into his coat buttons from his home in British-occupied Philadelphia to his brother at George Washington's camp.

Sandburg, Carl. *Abe Lincoln Grows Up.* Harcourt, 1985.

This is a classic biography of Lincoln, and selected chapters may be read aloud to students at this grade level.

Sanders, Scott. *Aurora Means Dawn.* Macmillan, 1989.

Pioneers begin to settle and establish a new and dawning land as recounted in this book.

Sandin, Joan. *The Long Way Westward.* Harper, 1989.

This easy-to-read text complements Sandin's earlier *The Long Way to a New Land* (Harper, 1986).

Santrey, Laurence. *Young Frederick Douglass: Fight for Freedom.* Troll, 1983.

This account of Douglass's life will acquaint readers with the childhood experiences that helped to shape the life of this slave who became a great abolitionist, journalist, and statesman.

Sewall, Marcia. *The Pilgrims of Plimoth.* Atheneum, 1986.

The daily lives and responsibilities of the pilgrim menfolk, womenfolk, and young folks who founded the Plymouth colony in 1620 are described in this book. Based on Governor William Bradford's writings, the text can be an introduction to primary source material.

Shub, Elizabeth. *The White Stallion.* Bantam, 1984.

This story of the white stallion is retold from Frank Dobie's *Tales of the Mustang.* Gretchen is saved by a mysterious stallion when she meets danger on the trail west in 1845.

Siegel, Beatrice. *Sam Ellis's Island.* Four Winds, 1985.

Sam Ellis, a Tory, acquired the small island in the year before the rebels signed a Declaration of Independence. This island has played an important role in American history.

Smith, Kathie Billingslea. *Martin Luther King, Jr.* Messner, 1987.

Like the other volumes in THE GREAT AMERICANS series, the strength of this book is in its use of authentic illustrations from the Smithsonian Institution and the National Portrait Gallery.

Spier, Peter. *We the People: The Constitution of the U.S.* Doubleday, 1987.

A line-by-line pictorial presentation of the preamble to the Constitution detailing the contrasting aspects of life in the 1700s and now. See also Spier's *The Star Spangled Banner* (Doubleday, 1986).

Stevenson, Augusta. *Paul Revere: Boston Patriot.* Scholastic, 1986.

The story of the revolutionary war patriot is told in this book.

Stone, Melissa. *Rebellion's Song.* Steck-Vaughn, 1989.

Six easily read biographies of colonial period notables are presented in attractive formats for third graders.

The Talking Eggs. Retold by Robert San Souci. Dial, 1989.

U.S. southern culture is depicted in this morality tale from the Creole South.

Tappan, Eva March. *American Hero Tales.* Houghton, 1934.

Long out of print, Tappan's works deserve republication, and her narrative style is worth emulating. This collection of biographical portraits contains suggestions for writing assignments. The text is suitable for reading aloud. This book is also usable at the fifth-grade level.

Tran-Khanh-Tuyet. *The Little Weaver of Thai-Yen Village.* San Francisco: Children's Book Press, 1987.

This is a story of a Vietnamese war orphan who comes to the United States. This book contains text written in both English and Vietnamese.

Weisgard, Leonard. *The Plymouth Thanksgiving.* Doubleday, 1967.

Weisgard's durable poem is based on Governor William Bradford's diary. Doubleday recently reissued the book in paperback.

Whelan, Gloria. *Next Spring an Oriole.* Random, 1987.

Libby Mitchell and her parents travel from Virginia in 1837 to settle in the forest near Saginaw, Michigan. An Indian girl becomes Libby's friend.

Winter, Jeanette. *Follow the Drinking Gourd.* Knopf, 1989.

Peg Leg Joe, a legendary one-legged sailor, teaches plantation slaves the way to freedom in the North with the lyrics of a song that contain directions to the Underground Railroad.

Grade Four:
California—
A Changing State

4.1   The Physical Setting: California and Beyond

Beck, Warren A., and Inez D. Haase. *Historical Atlas of California.* University of Oklahoma Press, 1975.

This is a usable resource for classroom reference.

Dana, Richard Henry. *Two Years Before the Mast.* Various paperback editions.

Excerpts from this classic (along with excerpts from Jack London's *Sea Wolf*) offer finely written descriptions of California's coastline, fog, and other physical features.

Fradin, Dennis. *California en Palabras y Fotos.* Children's Press, n.d.

The photographs and Spanish-language text in this book focus on contemporary California.

Magley, Beverly. *California Wildflowers.* Falcon Press, 1989.

This field guide to the state's most common flowers was prepared especially for children.

Morrison, Faye, and Kathryn Cusick. *Golden Poppies: California History and Contemporary Life in Books and Other Media for Young Readers—An Annotated Bibliography.* Library Professional Publications, 1987.

This is an extensive bibliography that can be a resource for fourth-grade teachers. The book's format is helpful for quick reference.

Pack, Janet. *California.* Watts, 1987.

This is an easy-to-read story of California that begins with the exploration, describes California's residents, and concludes with a discussion of California's modern problems and hoped-for solutions.

Rolle, Andrew F. *California: A History* (Fourth edition). Harlan Davidson, 1987.

Considered the standard history of California, this book begins with California's early inhabitants and covers Spanish rule, Mexican control, American exploration and settlement, the gold rush, immigration, and statehood. More than one quarter of the text is devoted to the twentieth century, including current issues. It is a useful teacher's resource.

Schneider, Bill, and D. D. Dowden. *The Tree Giants: The Story of the Redwoods, the World's Largest Trees.* Falcon Press, 1989.

One of California's most famous geographical features is discussed here for children's general knowledge and ecological consideration.

Siebert, Diane. *Mojave.* Crowell, 1988.

The beautiful illustrations and poetic text of this book portray the essence of the Mojave Desert.

4.2   Pre-Columbian Settlements and People

Bauer, Helen. *California Indian Days.* Doubleday, 1963.

The photos, line drawings, matrix, and researched text of this book tell of various California tribes. Once widely disseminated, this book is out of print. Bauer has written other books on gold rush, mission, and rancho days.

Cummins, Marjorie. *The Tache-Yokut Indians.* Pioneer Press (private publication). Order from the author, 2064 Carter Way, Hanford, CA 93230.

This is a useful teacher's resource and one of the few sources that deal with this central San Joaquin Valley tribe. *How Coyote Stole the Sun* is in preparation by the same author.

Curry, Jane Louise. *Back in the Before Time: Tales of the California Indians.* Macmillan, 1987.

The tales in this book are gathered from a number of California Indian tribes. They range from creation tales to the popular animal trickster tales.

de Angulo, Jamie. *Indian Tales.* Noonday Press, 1953.

The stories in this collection are drawn from folklore and mix fiction and fact.

Eargle, Dolan H. *The Earth Is Our Mother: A Guide to the Indians of California.* Trees Company Press, 1988.

This resource manual guides teachers to archeological sites, museums, and reservations. It includes festivals, powwows, and other events that are suitable for field trips within the state.

Faber, Gail, and Michele Lasagna. *Whispers from the First Californians.* Magpie Publications, 1981.

This teacher's resource contains authentic legends of California Indian culture.

Falk, Elsa. *Fog Island.* Wilcox & Follett, 1953.

Everyone called Ulam, a Chumash Indian boy, the "weak one" until he proved his strength and courage when he saved his chief's life. The setting is the Santa Barbara and Channel islands about 400 years ago.

Fisher, Anne B. *Stories California Indians Told.* Illustrated by Ruth Robbins. Parnassus, 1957.

Myths of California Indian storytellers are retold for children in this book. It deserves reprinting.

"The Grass on the Mountain," *Favorite Poems Old and New.* Translated by Mary Austin, edited by Helen Ferris. Doubleday, 1957.

Mary Austin was a California poet who revered native American Indian culture. Her treatment of this Paiute text has dignity and beauty.

Kroeber, Theodora. *Ishi, Last of His Tribe.* Bantam, 1973.

The lone survivor of the Yahi Indian tribe lived his life in fear of discovery by the white men who had exterminated his tribe. This book explores the thoughts of a peaceful people driven violently from the earth by white men.

Lee, Melicent. *Indian of the Oaks.* Acoma Books, n.d.

This is the story of a boy who lives among the Kumeyaay—Indians of the oaks. The San Diego Museum of Man sponsored the publication of this book.

Lyons, Grant. *Pacific Coast Indians of North America.* Messner, 1983.

The culture and history of the Tlinglit, Tsimshian, Kwaklutl, Salish, and other Indian peoples inhabiting the Pacific Coast from Alaska to California are discussed in this book.

Merrell, Leigh. *Tenach.* Nelson & Sons, 1954.

The adventures of a cabin boy of the *San Salvadore* on Cabrillo's exploration of the California coast in 1542—the sights of coastal California as they appeared through the eyes of a young boy—are recounted in this book.

Preble, Donna. *Yamino Kwiti: A Story of Indian Life in the Los Angeles Area.* Heydey Books, 1983.

First published in 1940, this novel deals with the conflicts between change and tradition. The customs, ways of life, and educational activities of these Indians are described.

Trafzer, Cliff, and Lee A. Smith-Trafzer. *Creation of a California Tribe: Grandfather's Maidu Indian Tales.* Sierra Oaks, 1988.

Tales of the Maidu Indians, told by a grandfather to schoolchildren, are included in this book.

4.3 Exploration and Colonial History

Erskine, Dorothy Ward. *Big Ride.* Crowell, 1958.

The first colonizing expedition to California from New Spain, led by Captain Anza in 1775, is seen through the experiences of young Pedro, his friend Jaime, and his family. They endure incredible hardships before reaching the present site of San Francisco.

Gilmore, N. Ray, and Gladys Gilmore. *Readings in California History.* Crowell, 1975.

Teachers will want to use excerpts from this invaluable collection of primary source material. It is worthy of republication.

Knill, Harry. *Early Los Angeles.* Bellerophon, 1984.

The brief clear text in this book, supplemented by paintings and drawings, presents a superb introduction to the early history of Los Angeles. This is an excellent source for information on costumes and early architecture. See also the author's *Story of Early California and Her Flags* (Bellerophon, 1984).

Lyngheim, Linda, and others. ***Father Junipero Serra: The Traveling Missionary.*** Langtry Publications, 1986.

The life of Father Junipero Serra is told accurately from his own diaries and letters. The brief chapters and direct writing style make this book accessible to all readers.

Roberts, Margaret. ***Pioneer California: Tales of Explorers, Indians and Settlers.*** Padre Productions, 1982.

A history of California exploration is told in this book as a series of stories that encompass the period from 1602 to 1865. Good pictures of Jedediah Smith, John C. Fremont, and John Sutter are included.

Terrell, John Upton. ***The Discovery of California.*** Harcourt, 1970.

The adventures of the first explorers of California are recounted in this book. Included are the search for the Northwest Passage, encounters with Indians along the Colorado River, and incidents with pirates.

4.4   Missions, Ranchos, and the Mexican War for Independence

The California Missions: A Pictorial History. Lane, 1979.

Historical photographs and drawings give readers a firsthand view of each mission and its development throughout the years. Maps, drawings, and reproductions of artwork and artifacts make this book especially useful to students who prepare reports on individual missions.

Coerr, Eleanor. ***The Bell Ringer and the Pirates.*** Harper, 1983.

Pio waits at the mission for the pirates to come, although his family, the padres, and the Indians have buried their belongings and run to the hills to hide. He waits to ring the bell to tell his people when it is safe to return to the mission. This book is based on a true incident at the Mission San Juan Capistrano.

Comstock, Esther J. ***Vallejo and the Four Flags.*** Comstock Bonanza Press, 1979.

Daily life on a hacienda and in the early settlements

along the Pacific coast is described in fascinating detail in this book. It is the story of young Mariano Guadalupe Vallejo and his life under the Spanish flag, the Mexican flag, the California flag, and finally under the flag of the United States of America.

Dutton, Davis. ***Missions of California.*** Ballantine, 1972.

This is a collection of writings, humorous pieces, and first-person and historical accounts collected from *Westways* magazine.

Faber, Gail, and Michele Lasagna. ***Whispers Along the Mission Trail.*** Magpie Publications, 1986.

"A story well told" describes this book and some of the narratives and visuals contained in this teacher's and classroom resource.

McMahan, Jackie. ***California Rancho Cooking.*** Olive Press, 1988.

This teacher's resource is useful for enlivening history in a "tasteful" manner.

Miller, Henry. ***Account of a Tour of the California Missions and Towns, 1856: The Journal and Drawings of Henry Miller.*** Bellerophon, 1989.

This first-person account of Henry Miller as he visited the missions scattered throughout California provides valuable insights into the appearance of the missions before their restoration in the twentieth century.

Montgomery, Jean. ***The Wrath of Coyote.*** Morrow, 1968.

This book depicts the Miwok Indians' resistance to Spanish settlers. It deserves republication.

O'Dell, Scott. ***Carlota.*** Houghton, 1977.

A young girl relates her feelings and experiences as a participant in the battle of San Pasqual during the last days of the war for possession of California. O'Dell's *Zia* and *Island of the Blue Dolphins* are worthwhile as well. Noguer of Spain publishes *La Isla de los Delfines Azules.*

Pinchot, Jane. ***Mexicans in America.*** Lerner, 1979.

This brief history of Mexicans in the United States covers their life in the American Southwest before statehood, the United States's acquisitions of their land, and the individual contributions of Mexicans to American life.

Politi, Leo. *Song of the Swallows.* Macmillan, 1986.

Juan rings the mission bells to welcome back the swallows to the San Juan Capistrano Mission in this story, set in the twentieth century. Politi's works include numerous titles that are usable throughout fourth grade (e.g., *The Mission Bell,* the story of Father Serra). All deserve republication.

4.5 Gold Rush, Statehood, and the Westward Movement

Beasley, Delilah. *Negro Trailblazers of California.* Greenwood reprint of 1969 original.

Despite its somewhat dated title, Beasley's work remains an important book for its topic. It is recommended as a resource for teachers.

Benet, Rosemary, and Stephen Vincent Benet. "Western Wagons," *A Book of Americans.* Holt, 1984.

This poem captures much of the spirit and attitude of the pioneers.

Bloch, Louis M., Jr. *Overland to California in 1859: A Guide for Wagon Train Travellers.* Bloch and Co., 1984.

Based exclusively on authentic source material, this guide contains advice on camping, marching, routing, dangers, and other aspects of overland travel by wagon train. The illustrations and maps are all authentic.

Blumberg, Rhoda. *The Great American Gold Rush.* Bradbury, 1989.

This account of the lives of ordinary people during gold rush days is a good source of pictures, sketches, and firsthand material, despite some inaccuracies.

Bulla, Clyde Robert. *The Secret Valley.* Crowell, 1949.

The Davis family of Missouri went to California in 1849 to find gold. In California, they thought their wishes might be fulfilled, and they were, in a very unexpected way.

The California Gold Rush. Photo Aids, 1988.

Included in this portfolio are 18 authentic, historic photographs and illustrations, ideal for classroom display. The grit and fiber of gold rush life come through in this primary source material.

California Women: Activities Guide, Kindergarten Through Grade Twelve. Prepared under the direction of Project SEE (Sex Equity in Education), California Department of Education, 1988.

This teacher's resource includes portraits of Biddy Mason and Bernarda Ruiz, two California women recommended for study in the *History–Social Science Framework.*

Chambers, Catherine. *California Gold Rush: Search for Treasure.* Troll, 1984.

Jake Fletcher thinks it will be just another ordinary day at Sutter's Mill—until James Marshall discovers gold!

Coerr, Eleanor. *Chang's Paper Pony.* Harper, 1988.

Set in California during the gold rush, this story of Chinese workers, if used at the fourth grade level, is best for low-level readers or students with limited English proficiency.

Dolan, Edward F., Jr. *Famous Builders of California.* Putnam, 1987.

Seven historical figures are covered in this book in short, readable chapters: Father Junipero Serra, John Fremont, John Sutter, Henry Wells, William Fargo, John Muir, and Luther Burbank. They represent adventurers, explorers, scientists, and businessmen important in California's history.

Epstein, Sam, and Beryl Epstein. *The Sacramento: Golden River of California.* Garrard, 1968.

The history of the Sacramento River is traced from early Spanish explorations through the gold rush era to the important role this river plays in contemporary California.

Fleischman, Sid. *By the Great Horn Spoon!* Atlantic Monthly Press, 1963.

Jack Flagg, an orphan, and his aunt's butler, Praiseworth, stow away on a ship bound for California. This book recounts their adventures aboard ship and in the gold rush of 1849. Alfaguara of Spain issues a Spanish-language version *¡Por la Gran Cuchara del Cuerno!* See also *Humbug Mountain* (Little, 1988) by the same author.

Flory, Jane. *The Golden Venture.* Houghton, 1976.

Minnike stows away on her father's wagon heading west from Missouri to join the California gold rush. While her father is looking for gold, Minnike has adventures of her own in San Francisco.

Garthwaite, Marian. *Coarsegold Gulch.* Doubleday, 1956.

This highly readable story of the rough'n'ready days of early California is worthy of republication, as are the author's *Holdup on Bootjack Hill* and *Shaken Days.*

Harvey, Brett. *Cassie's Journey: Going West in the 1860s.* Holiday, 1987.

A young girl relates the hardships and dangers of traveling with her family in a covered wagon from Illinois to California during the 1860s.

Hill, William E. *The California Trail Yesterday and Today.* Pruett Publishing Co., 1986.

Authentic photographs, sketches, and diary excerpts of the time offer usable primary-source material in this book. Teachers can use the excerpts for display. A detailed chronology of the history of the California Trail is provided.

Holliday, J. S. *The World Rushed In: The California Gold Rush Experience; An Eyewitness Account of a Nation Heading West.* Touchstone (Simon and Schuster), 1981.

Based on journals of an actual gold seeker, this book is valuable as a source of primary material or as a teacher's resource.

Katz, William L. *Black People Who Made the Old West.* Crowell, 1977.

These biographical sketches of 35 black men and women, including James Beckwourth, are laced with lively descriptions and amusing anecdotes.

Laurgaard, Rachel Kelly. *Patty Reed's Doll: The Story of the Donner Party.* Caxton Printers, 1989. Paperback reprints are available from Tomato Enterprises.

Based on actual happenings in the fateful Donner crossing of the Sierra in 1846, this story is told through the eyes of a small wooden doll that traveled from Illinois to California in young Patty Reed's pocket.

McCunn, Ruthanne L. *An Illustrated History of the Chinese in America.* Design Enterprises of San Francisco, 1979.

See also this author's picture book, *Pie-Biter,* which is based on a California legend and is available in English and Chinese.

McNeer, May. *The California Gold Rush.* Random, 1962.

This book is an account of the excitement, adventure, and lawlessness that followed the discovery of gold on John Sutter's farm in 1849.

Morrison, Dorothy. *Under a Strong Wind: The Adventures of Jessie Benton Fremont.* Atheneum, 1983.

This is a biography of Jessie Benton Fremont, a remarkable woman. The author uses primary sources in presenting Fremont's story.

Original Constitution of the State of California, 1849. Telefact Foundation, 1965.

A useful resource for teachers, this extraordinary book contains a facsimile of the original state constitution, which was issued in both Spanish and English. Edwin Klotz's introduction discusses the cultural confluence of the state in its birth years.

Stewart, George. *The Pioneers Go West.* Random, 1964.

An engrossing, easily read book that is based on the actual diary accounts of a young pioneer.

Trafzer, Clifford. *California's Indians and the Gold Rush.* Sierra Oaks, 1989.

This brief work enriches our pespective of a major period in California's history.

Uchida, Yoshiko. *Samurai of Gold Hill.* Creative Arts, 1985.

In 1869, twelve-year-old Kaichi journeys from Japan to California, where his father and his father's partners start a tea and silk farm.

4.6 The Period of Rapid Population Growth, Large-Scale Agriculture, and Linkage to the Rest of the United States

Beatty, Patricia. *Blue Stars Watching*. Morrow, 1969.

Resentful at being sent to California with his sister to avoid the dangers of the Civil War in Delaware, thirteen-year-old Will is soon entangled with Rebel plotters and Union spies in San Francisco. Beatty's *Eight Mules from Monterey* and *Me, California Perkins* are also recommended for this unit.

Cameron, Eleanor. *Julia and the Hand of God*. Dutton, 1977.

Eleven-year-old Julia Redfern wants to be a writer. She is deeply sensitive and often in trouble with her grandmother. A narrow escape from a forest fire that descends on Berkeley, California, in 1923 adds excitement. See also *That Julia Redfern* (Dutton, 1982) by the same author.

Donahue, Marilyn C. *The Valley in Between*. Walker, 1987.

A peaceful farming community in the San Bernardino Valley is transformed into a lawless frontier town by the recall of Mormons to Utah, Indian raids, the discovery of gold in the mountains, and pre–Civil War feelings.

Gates, Doris. *Elderberry Bush*. Viking, 1960.

This is a significant work that deserves republication; it is a simple, human interest story of young girls growing up in the Santa Clara Valley during the early 1900s. Turn-of-the-century San Jose is depicted in one episode.

Lapp, Rudolph. *Afro-Americans in California*. Materials for Today's Learnings, 1987.

Available in paperback, Lapp's work offers history and commentary that is valuable for teachers' own reading.

Levine, Ellen. *If You Lived at the Time of the Great San Francisco Earthquake*. Scholastic, 1987.

This book is written in a question-and-answer format with stories included to personalize the answers. It will answer many questions children have about the earthquake.

Reinstedt, Randall A. *More Than Memories: History and Happenings of the Monterey Peninsula*. Ghost Town Publishers, 1985.

Particularly helpful in this book are the chapters on California in the late nineteenth and twentieth centuries. Excellent black and white photographs are included.

Uchida, Yoshiko. *A Jar of Dreams*. Macmillan, 1981.

This story of the Great Depression era is told by eleven-year-old Rinko, the only girl in a Japanese-American family living in Oakland. It portrays the tensions and problems of that time.

Uncle John's Stories for Good California Children. Facsimile reprint. Reprinted by California Kids History Catalogue, Sonoma, Calif.

A curiosity piece, this tiny paperback shows literary entertainment for young people, circa 1860. This was the first book of children's stories to be published in California during the American period. It includes tales from such lands as Java, New England, and China.

Wilder, Laura Ingalls. *West from Home: Letters of Laura Ingalls Wilder to Almanzo Wilder, San Francisco, 1915*. Edited by Roger Lea MacBride. Harper, 1974.

When this noted children's author was a struggling journalist, she visited San Francisco and the Panama Pacific International Exposition. Though beyond the reading level of some fourth graders, the letters in this collection provide opportunities for reading aloud from a primary source or for collaborative group discussions.

Wong, Don, and Irene Dea Collier. *Chinese Americans, Past and Present*. Association of Chinese Teachers, 1977 (available from distributors).

The emphasis on work sheets in this booklet is a drawback, but usable stories, primary sources, and other material are included in this teacher's resource.

Yee, Paul. *Tales from Gold Mountain*. Macmillan, 1989.

The history of brave Chinese immigrants is the basis for this collection of authentic folktales. The stories are unusual and strikingly illustrated.

Yep, Laurence. ***Dragonwings.*** Harper, 1977.

Windrider and his son, Moon Shadow, endure poverty, the mockery of other Chinese, and the longing for the rest of the family in China to make a dream come true—creating a dragonlike flying machine. A vivid picture of San Francisco's Chinatown in the early 1900s is presented in this book. See also *Child of the Owl* and *The Rainbow People* by the same author.

4.7   Modern California: Immigration, Technology, and Cities

Beatty, Patricia. ***The Queen's Own Grove.*** Morrow, 1966.

In the 1880s, young Amelia Bromfield-Brown moves from Canada to Riverside, California, where her family buys an orange grove.

Climo, Shirley. ***City! San Francisco.*** Macmillan, 1990.

George Ancona's photographs are an impressive addition to this city's tale. The author traces the city's development from early days to the present, enabling fourth graders to develop a better awareness of one of California's major cities.

Franchere, Ruth. ***Cesar Chavez.*** Harper, 1988.

In this biography of the leader of the United Farm Workers Association, simple language relates Chavez's part in the struggle to improve the conditions of farm workers.

Gates, Doris. ***Blue Willow.*** Viking, 1940.

Janey, the daughter of a migrant worker, dreams of finding a permanent home and a mantle for her cherished blue willow plate. Set in the San Joaquin Valley, the book touches on the need for beauty, property, and place.

Healton, Sarah, and Dick Hackbert. ***California, So Wondrous to Behold.*** California Reading Association, 1980.

This 18-page choral reading can be a good capstone for the year's study in this unit.

Lee, Gregory. ***Los Angeles, California.*** Crestwood House, 1989.

This is a colorful, nonfiction work that depicts contemporary California culture.

Leopold, A. Starker, et al. ***Wild California: Vanishing Lands, Vanishing Wildlife.*** University of California Press, 1985.

The photographs in this book are worthwhile in discussing change, conservation, and the environment.

Pelta, Kathy. ***Bridging the Golden Gate.*** Lerner, 1987.

This book captures the ambition and excitement of a great engineering effort. It includes numerous fascinating black-and-white photographs and a chart of facts and figures.

Perl, Lila, and Alma F. Ada. ***Piñatas and Paper Flowers—Piñatas y flores de papel: Holidays of the Americas in English and Spanish.*** Clarion, 1983.

This well-illustrated book contains "how-to" information on the various holidays celebrated in the countries of Central and South America.

Stagecoach Santa. Retold by Randall A. Reinstedt. Ghost Town Publishers, 1986.

This work is a diverting piece of California lore, traced to the late 1940s but set in pioneer days. Reinstedt's *Otters, Octupuses and Odd Creatures of the Deep* (Ghost Town, 1987) touches on geographical features of contemporary California.

Uchida, Yoshiko. ***Journey Home.*** Macmillan, 1982.

On her family's release from Topaz Concentration Camp, Yuki tries to adjust to a new treatment of Japanese-Americans during World War II. See also Uchida's *Journey to Topaz* (Creative Arts Books, 1985).

Grade Five: U.S. History and Geography— Making a New Nation

5.1   The Land and People Before Columbus

Baylor, Byrd. *And It Is Still That Way.* Scribner, 1976.
American Indian children retell more than 40 legends in contemporary language. This book is worthy of republication.

Bulla, Clyde Robert. *Viking Adventure.* Crowell, 1963.
Sigurd, son of Olaf the Strong, sails in a Viking ship on a long and perilous voyage to Vinland.

Caduto, Michael J., and Joseph Bruhac. *Keepers of the Earth: Native American Stories and Environmental Activities for Children.* Fulcrum, Inc., 1988.
Content that involves several subject areas makes this collection of native American stories and environmental activities a helpful teacher's resource and a practical compendium.

Esbensen, Barbara Juster. *Ladder to the Sky.* Little, Brown, 1989.
The use of herbs and plants for medicinal purposes is given a legendary base in this retelling of an Ojibway folktale.

Guard, Jean, and Ray A. Williamson. *They Dance in the Sky: Native American Star Myths.* Houghton, 1987.
Native Americans have watched the night sky for countless years and have told stories of the constellations and stars. This book is a fascinating collection of some of these tales.

Hetmann, Frederick. *Historias de Pieles Rojas.* Madrid: Alfaguara, 1985.
This book features stories in Spanish about Navajo, Apache, and Hopi Indian children.

Historical Atlas of the United States. National Geographic Society, 1989.
This comprehensive atlas of U.S. history presents a geographic perspective. Thematic sections include the land, people, boundaries, economy, networks, and communities.

Hunt, W. Ben. *The Complete How-to Book of Indian Craft.* Collier, 1973.
The format of this book is appealing to students, as is Hunt's *Indian Crafts and Lore* (Golden Press, 1954). Both books are out of print and deserve republication.

Lauber, Patricia. *Who Discovered America? Settlers and Explorers of the New World Before the Time of Columbus.* Random, 1970.
This scientific detective story shows how specialists investigate clues to fill in the story of the New World before the time of Christopher Columbus.

Lomask, Milton. *Great Lives: Exploration.* Scribner, 1988.
This is a good resource work for its topic.

McClard, Megan, and George Ypsilantis. *Hiawatha and the Iroquois League.* Silver Burdett, 1989.
Though the reading level may be beyond that of some fifth graders, this book contains valuable information about the Hiawatha legend, the Iroquois, and European settlers.

McEvedy, Colin. *The Penguin Atlas of North American History to 1870.* Penguin, 1986.
This historical atlas can be a boon for classroom research and an enriching resource.

Magnusson, Magness, and Herman Pallson. *Vinland Sagas and Norse Discovery of America.* Penguin, 1965.
The epic quality of this era is reflected in this book. Good background information is provided.

Martin, Paul. *Indians Before Columbus: Twenty Thousand Years of North American History Revealed by Archaeology.* University of Chicago Press, 1975.
This scholarly work is perhaps best used as a

teacher's resource, although its pictures can be beneficial to students.

Mayo, Gretchen Will. *Earthmaker's Tales: North American Indian Stories About Earth Happenings.* Walker, 1989.

Fog, snow, wind, and volcanoes are explained in this collection of American Indian myths. The book includes background information on the sources as well as a helpful glossary. See also *Star Tales* by the same author.

Schiller, Barbara. *The Vinlanders' Saga.* Holt, 1966.

This saga deals with the discovery and exploration of North America 500 years before Christopher Columbus.

Sneve, Virginia Driving Hawk. *Dancing Teepees: Poems of American Indian Youth.* Holiday, 1989.

This book includes ancient and contemporary poems and songs with illustrations similar in style to traditional Indian art.

"A Song of Greatness," in *Favorite Poems Old and New.* Translated by Mary Austin; edited by Helen Ferris. Doubleday, 1957.

This Chippewa song text is short and easily enjoyed by fifth graders.

Trease, Geoffrey. *Viking's Sunset.* Criterion, 1961.

Harold sails his longboat to the shores of Lake Superior. This book conveys the vast scope of early Vikings' travels.

Tunis, Edwin. *Indians.* Crowell, 1979.

Still worthwhile after 30 years, this book contains sketches and a discussion of Indians' tools and customs.

Weinstein-Farson, Laurie. *The Wampanoag.* Chelsea House, 1989.

The culture and history of this North American Indian tribe are depicted in this book.

Yue, Charlotte. *The Tipi: A Center of Native American Life.* Knopf, 1984.

The tipi was a sophisticated dwelling developed by the plains Indians to meet the demands of their harsh life on the Great Plains. See also *The Pueblo* (Houghton, 1955) by David Yue and Charlotte Yue.

Ziter, Cary B. *The Moon of Falling Leaves: The Great Buffalo Hunt.* Illustrated by Gretchen Will Mayo. Watts, 1988.

The buffalo was the essential element in the life of the plains Indians. This book depicts the cycle of hunting and herding and the use of skins and meat for survival.

5.2   The Age of Exploration

Baker, Betty. *Walk the World's Rim.* Harper, 1965.

Chaklo, an Indian boy, travels from what is now Texas to Mexico City in the sixteenth century with a black slave, Esteban; Cabeza de Vaca; and two other Spanish explorers. See also *A Stranger and Afraid* (Macmillan, 1972).

Blackwood, Alan. *Ferdinand Magellan.* Bookwright, 1986.

The story of Magellan's voyage from Spain to the Pacific and the first circumnavigation of the world is told in this book.

Bulla, Clyde, and Michael Syson. *Conquista.* Crowell, 1978.

How did Indians acquire their first horses? Francisco Coronado's expedition into North America, described in this book, is one possible way.

Columbus and the Age of Exploration. Illustrated by Ken Stott. Watts, 1985.

An overview of Christopher Columbus and other explorers ranging from Vasco da Gama to Francis Drake is provided in this book. Life on the sea and the motivations for exploring are well described.

Fritz, Jean. *Brendan the Navigator: A History Mystery About the Discovery of America.* Putnam, 1979.

This book portrays the life of Saint Brendan and chronicles his legendary voyage to North America, a voyage made long before the Vikings arrived. See also Fritz's *Where Do You Think You're Going, Christopher Columbus?* (Putnam, 1980).

Goodnough, David. *Francis Drake, Sea Pirate.* Troll, 1979.

An account of the life of the famous English navigator is given in this book.

Grosseck, Joyce, and Elizabeth Attwood. *Great Explorers.* Gateway Press, 1988.

In this book, black-and-white photos illustrate biographical chapters on various explorers. This reprint is a possible resource for students' research or for students with special interest in the topic.

Humble, Richard. *The Age of Leif Erikson.* Watts, 1989.

With a time line and a brief discussion, this picture book provides background and sets the European exploration in perspective.

Levinson, Nancy Smiler. *Christopher Columbus: Voyager to the Unknown.* Lodestar, 1990.

An engaging narrative in this book presents new views of the great explorer, but the reading level is above that of most fifth graders. Clear maps and primary source material make this book a good reference for teachers and students.

The Log of Christopher Columbus' First Voyage to America: In the Year 1492, as Copied Out in Brief by Bartholomew Las Casas. Transcribed by Bartholomew Las Casas. Linnet Books, 1989.

Columbus's log was "copied out in brief" by his companion. The accompanying illustrations, signatures, maps, and so forth make this an excellent primary source for fifth graders.

Matthews, Rupert. *The Voyage of Columbus.* Bookwright, 1989.

This book is amply illustrated with an inviting format and an easily followed narrative.

O'Dell, Scott. *The King's Fifth.* Houghton, 1966.

This adventure story is told through the reminiscences of Francisco Coronado's fifteen-year-old cartographer.

Soule, Gardner. *Christopher Columbus on the Great Sea of Darkness.* Watts, 1988.

This book describes the voyages of Columbus and details the events and discoveries connected with each.

Stein, R. Conrad. *The Story of Marquette and Jolliet.* Children's Press, 1981.

One of the CORNERSTONES OF FREEDOM series, this book is brief and easily read.

Syme, Ronald. *De Soto, Finder of the Mississippi.* Morrow, 1957.

The adventures of Hernando de Soto in the New World are told in this book. He was with Francisco Pizarro in Peru and later led an expedition from Florida to Oklahoma, discovering the Mississippi River en route. See also *Henry Hudson, La Salle of the Mississippi, Columbus: Finder of the New World,* and *Magellan: First Around the World,* all by the same author.

5.3 Settling the Colonies

Bailey, Thomas A., and David M. Kennedy. *The American Spirit, Volume I.* Heath, 1987.

Though intended for much older readers, this collection of primary sources provides some material that can be used in the fifth grade; e.g., statements by William Bradford, Anne Hutchinson, and Thomas Phillips. This volume is useful as a teacher's resource.

Book of Great American Documents. Edited by Vincent Wilson, Jr. American History Research Associates, 1987.

This teacher's resource is an impressive collection of primary sources. See also Wilson's *Book of Distinguished American Women* and *Book of Founding Fathers.*

Conneau, Theophile. *A Slaver's Log Book: Twenty Years' Residence in Africa.* Avon, 1982.

This book presents journal entries, memoranda, and conversations by a slave-ship captain. It is presently available in paperback.

Fisher, Leonard Everett. *The Homemakers.* Watts, 1973.

Beautiful illustrations and clear, concise text describe how the four staples of every colonial home—candles, soap, brooms, and cider—were made.

Hargrove, Julia. THE PRIMARY SOURCE. Perfection Form, 1987.

Although the emphasis is on work sheets and answer keys, this series contains useful material. Multiple volumes deal with different periods in American history. This teacher's resource should be used selectively and discriminately.

Knight, James. ADVENTURES IN COLONIAL AMERICA. Troll, 1982.

This set of handy paperbacks is easily read. Multiple copies of selected titles can be used for classroom cooperative assignments. These books are better suited to classrooms than to libraries.

Lawson, Robert. *Ben and Me, Benjamin Franklin as Written by His Good Mouse Amos.* Little, Brown, 1939.

Amos, a close friend and constant companion of Ben Franklin, finally reveals that he, a mouse, was the one really responsible for Ben's inventions and successes.

McGovern, Ann. *If You Lived in Colonial Times.* Scholastic, 1969.

This informative and entertaining book offers an unusual approach to the study of life during the colonial period in the United States.

Madison, Arnold. *How the Colonists Lived.* David McKay, 1980.

The text and drawings in this book depict the lives of the colonists: their struggles for survival; unexpected dangers they faced; their efforts to obtain food and clothing; and their homes, villages, furniture, tools, weapons, utensils, and modes of travel.

Tunis, Edwin. *Colonial Living.* Crowell, 1976.

Colonial era clothes, houses, and furniture are simply explained and vividly illustrated in this book, which provides a "how did it work" guide to seven-teenth- and eighteenth-century America. See also *Tavern at the Ferry* (Crowell, 1973) by the same author.

Williams, Selma. *Demeter's Daughters: The Women Who Founded America, 1587–1787.* Atheneum, 1976.

The roles of women in the colonial period from presettlement times to the Federal era are described in this book. Included in this teacher's resource are such fields as agriculture, politics, journalism, and business.

5.3.1 The Virginia Settlement

Africa Remembered: Narratives by West Africans from the Era of the Slave Trade. Edited by Philip D. Curtin. University of Wisconsin Press, 1967.

A valuable work of primary source material, this book is currently available in both hardback and softback editions.

Anderson, Joan. *A Williamsburg Household.* Clarion, 1988.

Events in the household of a slave-holding white family in colonial Williamsburg are the focus of this book.

Benezet, Anthony. *Views of American Slavery, Taken a Century Ago.* Ayer, 1969.

This reprint contains observations of the enslaving, importing, and purchasing of Africans in 1760.

Bulla, Clyde Robert. *A Lion to Guard Us.* Crowell, 1981.

This is an easily read novel of three youngsters' perilous journey to the Virginia colony.

Campbell, Elizabeth. *Jamestown: The Beginning.* Little, Brown, 1974.

Writing from the points of view of the settlers, the ship's crew, the American Indians, and the captain of the expedition, the author of this book conveys the suspense of the voyage and the sailors' joy and thankfulness at the long-awaited sighting of land.

Fritz, Jean. *The Double Life of Pocahontas.* Putnam, 1983.

This biography of the famous native American

emphasizes her adulation of John Smith and the roles she played in two different cultures.

Hilton, Suzanne. *The World of Young George Washington.* Walker, 1987.

The childhood and youth of George Washington in the context of Virginia's society in the eighteenth century are described in this book.

Kupperman, Karen O. *Captain John Smith: A Select Edition of His Writings.* University of North Carolina Press, 1988.

This teacher's resource and background book is part of the INSTITUTE OF EARLY AMERICAN HISTORY AND CULTURE series.

Latham, Jean Lee. *This Dear-Bought Land.* Harper, 1957.

This is an outstanding story of Captain John Smith and the settlement of Jamestown.

Meltzer, Milton. *The Black Americans: A History in Their Own Words.* Crowell, 1987.

Meltzer brings together an extensive selection of primary sources, several of which complement this unit's examination of slavery. This book is useful for other units and topics as well.

O'Dell, Scott. *The Serpent Never Sleeps: A Novel of Jamestown and Pocahontas.* Houghton, 1987.

This novel transports the reader from a lavish seventeenth-century English castle across the Atlantic to a shipwreck off Bermuda and finally to the struggling early settlements at Jamestown.

5.3.2 Life in New England

Bradford, William. *Of Plymouth Plantation, 1620–1647.* Edited by Samuel E. Morison. Knopf, 1952.

This primary source consists of Governor William Bradford's own documentation of his colony's history and is a useful teacher's resource.

Bulla, Clyde Robert. *John Billington: Friend of Squanto.* Crowell, 1956.

John is captured by Indians in the beginning days of Plymouth Colony but is released when Squanto intervenes. The same tribe of Indians later helps the colonists celebrate the first Thanksgiving. See also *Squanto: Friend of the Pilgrims* (Scholastic, 1988) by the same author.

Clapp, Patricia C. *Constance: A Story of Early Plymouth.* Penguin, 1986.

Told in the form of a diary, this is the story of Constance, a fourteen-year-old member of the Mayflower Company. Hardships and joys experienced by the first settlers are vividly pictured. Portions of this book can be easily excerpted for classroom use. See also *Witches' Children: A Story of Salem* (Penguin, 1987) by the same author.

Dubowski, Cathy East. *The Story of Squanto, First Friend of the Pilgrims.* Dell, 1990.

A native American researcher for the Plimoth Plantation museum recommends this book as a "step toward revealing the importance of the native presence in New England history." This moving biography is not difficult or lengthy and would be worthwhile for class reading.

Field, Rachel. *Calico Bush.* Macmillan, 1987.

On her grandmother's sudden death, a young girl becomes indentured to a Massachusetts family during the French and Indian Wars. A fine story of survival and hardship that is possibly better suited for advanced readers, this book is usable at the eighth-grade level as well.

Fisher, Margaret, and Mary Jane Fowler. *Colonial America: English Colonies.* Gateway Press, 1988.

This reprint centers on daily life in the New England colonies. It contains black-and-white photographs and reproductions of paintings.

Fritz, Jean. *Who's That Stepping on Plymouth Rock?* Coward, 1975.

One of America's most visible patriotic symbols, one with an unusually checkered history, now rests under a monument on the waterfront in Plymouth, Massachusetts. Numerous titles by Fritz are appropriate for this grade; e.g., *The Cabin Faced West* (Penguin, 1987).

Hawthorne, Nathaniel. *True Stories from History and Biography.* (Volume 6 of the CENTENARY EDITION OF THE

WORKS OF NATHANIEL HAWTHORNE.) Ohio State University Press, 1972.

This is a trove of worthwhile material, especially the "Grandfather's Chair" stories of Puritan New England. Recommended for reading aloud and as a background resource, it includes glimpses of the lives of Roger Williams, Anne Hutchinson, Ben Franklin, and others.

Homes in the Wilderness: A Pilgrim's Journal of Plymouth Plantation in 1620 by William Bradford and Others of the Mayflower Company. Edited by Margaret Wise Brown. Linnet Books, 1988.

This simplified version of *Mourt's Relation,* a primary source from the Plymouth colony, is also available in paperback.

Hooks, William. *The Legend of the White Doe.* Macmillan, 1988.

This is a tale about the fate of Virginia Dare, the first English child born in the New World.

Krensky, Stephen. *Witch Hunt: It Happened in Salem Village.* Random, 1989.

The drama and terror of the Salem witch trials come through in this easily read narrative. The book is recommended for independent reading by students.

Loeper, John J. *Going to School in 1776.* Atheneum, 1973.

This book depicts later life in the colonies and is a good source for the "school enactment" described in the *History–Social Science Framework.*

Monjo, F. N. *The House on Stink Alley.* Illustrated by Robert Quackenbush. Holt, 1977.

Eight-year-old Brewster tells the story of the Pilgrims' stay in Holland before they emigrated to America. His father, William Brewster, is bitter toward King James, and much tension is involved.

Mourt's Relation. Edited by Dwight B. Heath. Applewood Books, 1986.

This daily journal of the Pilgrims' first winter was written by members of the Plymouth colony and published in England in 1622. It is a useful teacher's resource. See also *Homes in the Wilderness* in this unit.

The Oxford Book of Children's Verse in America. Edited by Donald Hall. Oxford University Press, 1985.

Hall's collection includes excerpts from *The Bay Psalm Book* and *The New England Primer,* both of which are usable in this unit. Teachers of the fifth and eighth grades will discover that this material can complement other units as well.

Perl, Lila. *Slumps, Grunts, and Snickerdoodles: What Colonial America Ate and Why.* Clarion Books, 1979.

This is a history of American colonial victuals.

Siegel, Beatrice. *Fur Trappers and Traders: The Indians, the Pilgrims and the Beaver.* Walker, 1987.

The critical importance of the fur trade to the settlement and survival of the colonists is discussed in this book. This trade led to conflicts among groups who vied for the riches it offered and opened the way to westward expansion.

Sloane, Eric. *An ABC Book of Early Americana.* Doubleday, 1963.

This is a fine resource for showing the everyday work, tools, and toys of early America. It includes clear, engaging sketches and deserves republication.

Speare, Elizabeth. *Sign of the Beaver.* Houghton, 1983.

This is the story of the friendship between a young white settler in Maine, left on his own while his father goes to get their family, and a young Indian who helps the young settler survive.

The Thanksgiving Primer. Plimoth Plantation, Inc., 1987.

The most commonly asked questions regarding the first Thanksgiving are answered in this book.

Wisler, G. Clifton. *This New Land.* Walker, 1987.

The story of the Pilgrims' journey on the *Mayflower* and their life in the new colony is recounted in this book.

Ziner, Feenie. *Squanto.* Linnet Books, 1988.

This biography relies on primary source documents and portrays European colonization from the native American's viewpoint. Portions might be read aloud to fifth graders or used by teachers for background information.

5.3.3 The Middle Colonies

Cousins, Margaret. *Ben Franklin of Old Philadelphia.* Random, 1963.

Long a favorite with young readers, this book joins Ingri D'Aulaire and Edgar P. Parin's *Benjamin Franklin* (Doubleday, 1987) as a source for fifth graders who are interested in the Philadelphia patriot.

Dolson, Hildegarde. *William Penn.* Random, 1963.

This biography is worthy of republication.

Franklin, Benjamin. *Poor Richard's Almanack.* Peter Pauper Press, n.d.

There are many editions of this remarkable collection of the wit and wisdom of Ben Franklin. It is a delightful volume of brief, pithy sayings. See also *The Autobiography of Benjamin Franklin* in various paperback editions.

Fritz, Jean. *What's the Big Idea, Ben Franklin?* Putnam, 1982.

Franklin's extraordinary endeavors, inventions, and personality are delightfully presented here.

The Legend of Sleepy Hollow. Retold by Robert San Souci. Doubleday, 1986.

Daniel San Souci's illustrations for this Washington Irving tale are superb portrayals of everyday life in the middle colonies.

Rip Van Winkle. Retold and illustrated by John Howe. Little, Brown, 1988.

Washington Irving's tale of the Catskills is given fine treatment here. Howe's version is probably easier for most fifth graders to follow. Save Irving's original for use in the eighth grade.

5.4   Settling the Trans-Appalachian West

Anderson, Joan. *Pioneer Children of Appalachia.* Clarion, 1986.

This is a contemporary re-creation of the life of nineteenth-century Appalachian settlers. Actors in the re-creation were photographed at Fort New Salem, a living-history museum in West Virginia. The black-and-white photographic essay is a portrait of an extended pioneer family.

Brown, John Mason. *Daniel Boone: The Opening of the Wilderness.* Random, 1952.

One of the *Landmark Series*, the book is a good one for reading aloud. It is out of print.

Daugherty, James. *Daniel Boone.* Viking, 1939.

Possibly better suited for advanced readers, this biography presents a vivid account of this trailblazer and hero. It deserves republication.

Edmonds, Walter D. *The Matchlock Gun.* Putnam, 1941.

This true story, told as fiction, is a faithful depiction of the minds and spirits of Dutch settlers in colonial New York amidst French and Indian invasions in 1756. Although Nathaniel Benchley's *Small Wolf* (Harper, 1972) is intended for younger children, it is a good foil for this novel.

Lawlor, Laurie. *Daniel Boone.* Whitman, 1989.

This is a biography of the great American frontiersman.

Marrin, Albert. *Struggle for a Continent: The French and Indian Wars, 1690–1760.* Macmillan, 1987.

The historical importance of these wars is made clear in this book, which is written in the manner of a well-told story. A good teacher's resource, this book is perhaps best suited for more mature fifth graders.

Steele, William O. *Daniel Boone's Echo.* Harcourt, 1957.

This collection offers folktales and legends surrounding Daniel Boone and the Appalachians of his time. It is out of print.

Stevenson, Augusta. *Daniel Boone: Young Hunter and Tracker.* Aladdin Books, 1961.

This paperback is an easily read biography that is within the abilities of most fifth graders.

5.5   The War for Independence

Akers, Charles. *Abigail Adams: An American Woman.* Scott, Foresman, 1980.

An intimate portrait of an extraordinary woman and a compelling account of the political, social, and intellectual currents during the birth and formative years of a nation are provided in this useful teacher's reference.

Baker, Charles F., III. *The Struggle for Freedom: Plays on the American Revolution.* Cobblestone, 1990.

This softcover book of plays includes maps of the historical sites mentioned and resource material for teachers.

Brady, Esther Wood. *Toliver's Secret.* Crown, 1988.

During the revolutionary war, ten-year-old Ellen Toliver is asked by her grandfather to substitute for him and carry secret messages through British lines to a waiting courier.

Clapp, Patricia. *I'm Deborah Sampson: A Soldier in the War of the Revolution.* Lothrop, 1977.

The childhood, war experience, and later marriage and family life of the young woman who disguised herself as a man to fight in the American Revolution are recounted by Deborah Sampson herself in this book. The book is worthy of republication.

Collier, James L., and Christopher Collier. *My Brother Sam Is Dead.* Macmillan, 1985.

This book presents a grim view of the revolution in Connecticut as seen by Tim Meeker, who is unable to accept either the convictions of his Tory parents or those of his "rebel" brother, Sam. See also *Jump Ship to Freedom* (Delacorte, 1981) and *War Comes to Willy Freeman* (Delacorte, 1983) by the same authors.

Davis, Burke. *Black Heroes of the American Revolution.* Harcourt, 1976.

This book is a tribute to the black heroes and to the countless others who fought gallantly in the American Revolution in hope of winning their own independence.

Emerson, Ralph Waldo. "Concord Hymn," in *Favorite Poems Old and New.* Edited by Helen L. Ferris. Doubleday, 1957.

Ferris's popular collection also contains such classics as Felicia Hemans' "Landing of the Pilgrim Fathers" and Joaquin Miller's "Columbus." This poem is recommended in the *History–Social Science Framework.*

Evans, Elizabeth. *Weathering the Storm: Women of the Revolution.* Scribner, 1975.

The journal entries of 11 women cover household life during the Revolution. This book is a useful index to persons, places, and subjects, such as women in the army, Indians, and medicines.

Forbes, Esther. *Johnny Tremain.* Houghton, 1943.

This is a famous, enduring work of exciting historical fiction. Though recommended for reading aloud at the fifth grade level, it is also applicable for grade eight. Forbes's *Paul Revere and the World He Lived In* (Houghton, 1972) is an excellent background book for teachers.

Fritz, Jean. *Shh! We're Writing the Constitution.* Putnam, 1987.

In this book, Fritz juxtaposes the historical background with the varying personalities of the delegates to the Constitutional Convention.

Gauch, Patricia Lee. *This Time, Tempe Wick?* Coward, 1974.

Based on a revolutionary war legend about a real girl, this story tells how Tempe Wick helped feed and clothe the thousands of American soldiers who spent the winters of 1780 and 1781 in Jockey Hollow, New Jersey.

Giblin, James Cross. *Fireworks, Picnics and Flags: The Story of the Fourth of July Symbols.* Clarion, 1983.

History and culture come together in a book that can be used by both teachers and students.

Kent, Zachary. *George Washington.* Children's Press, 1986.

This is an easily read biography.

Knight, James E. *Boston Tea Party, Rebellion in the Colonies.* Troll, 1982.

A Boston merchant describes the American colonists' act of protest against British taxation and the tea monopoly of the East India Co. See also *The Winter at Valley Forge, Survival & Victory* (Troll, 1982) by the same author.

Lawson, Robert. *Mr. Revere and I.* Little, Brown, 1953.

This is an account of certain episodes in the life of Paul Revere as revealed by his horse, Scheherazade.

Levy, Elizabeth. *If You Were There When They Signed the Constitution.* Scholastic, 1987.

An introduction to the Constitution is provided in this book. Included are the document's background, profiles of delegates to the Constitutional Convention, compromises made at the convention, and an explanation of the mechanism provided to change the Constitution.

Longfellow, Henry Wadsworth. "Paul Revere's Ride," in *Selected Poems.* Penguin Classic (paperback), 1988.

This collection contains the entire unabridged ballad. Ted Rand's illustrated version is published by Dutton and effectively catches the mood of the poem. Longfellow's "Hiawatha's Childhood" is usable in earlier units.

Maestro, Betsy. *A More Perfect Union: The Story of Our Constitution.* Lothrop, 1987.

An appealing account of the long, hot Philadelphia summer of 1787 is given in this book.

Martin, J. P. *Private Yankee Doodle.* Edited by George Scheer. Eastern Acorn Press reprint, 1962.

"Being a narrative of the dangers and sufferings of a Revolutionary soldier," this journal could be excerpted for its firsthand accounts. The book is a useful teacher's resource.

Millender, Dharathula H. *Crispus Attucks: Black Leader of Colonial Patriots.* Macmillan, 1983.

First issued as a part of Bobbs-Merrill's *Childhood of Famous Americans* series, this biography has been popular with young readers. It is available in paperback.

Patterson, Charles. *Thomas Jefferson.* Watts, 1987.

A dry but informative account of this guardian of liberty is provided in this book.

Peterson, Helen S. *Abigail Adams: Dear Partner.* Garrard, 1967.

Recently reissued, this slim biography is good reading. Peterson quotes many revealing excerpts from Adams's own writings and statements.

Phelan, Mary Kay. *The Story of the Boston Massacre.* Crowell, 1976.

Colonial Boston comes alive in historical dramas. They mix authenticity with vivid descriptions of one of the most crucial moments in American history. See also *The Story of the Boston Tea Party,* illustrated by Keith Neely (Crowell, 1973).

Reische, Diana. *Patrick Henry.* Watts, 1987.

This book is a worthy companion to Charles Patterson's book on Jefferson.

Richmond, Merle. *Phillis Wheatley.* Chelsea House, 1988.

Although better suited for older readers, this engrossing biography contains primary source material that teachers may excerpt and use.

Stevenson, Augusta. *Molly Pitcher: Young Patriot.* Macmillan, 1986.

The courage of this heroine during the American War of Independence is related in this book.

Stone, Melissa. *Rebellion's Song.* Steck-Vaughn, 1989.

The book includes easily read biographical portraits of Paul Revere, Nathan Hale, Phillis Wheatley, Abigail Adams, and other colonists who were engaged in the great turmoil. It is one of the *Moments in American History* series.

Sutton, Felix. *The How and Why Wonder Book of the American Revolution.* Price Stern Sloan, 1985.

This is an easy-to-use book for fifth graders. Sutton's *How and Why of North American Indians* is a companion volume that is usable in other units.

Wheatley, Phillis. "Should You, My Lord," in *Imaginary Gardens*. Compiled by Charles Sullivan. Harry Abrams, 1989.

This noteworthy poem, written by a black slave, provides opportunity for discussion by students.

Wibberley, Leonard. *John Treegate's Musket*. Farrar, 1959.

Peter Treegate is apprenticed at the age of eleven years and separated from his father. He soon sees a Boston he had never known existed. The story is set just before the American Revolution.

5.6   Life in the Young Republic

Alcott, Louisa May. *An Old-Fashioned Thanksgiving*. Holiday, 1989.

This little-known work was first penned for a nineteenth-century magazine and is real Americana. It is illustrated with wood engravings.

Bealer, Alex. *Only the Names Remain: The Cherokees and the Trail of Tears*. Little, Brown, 1972.

This book describes the life of the Cherokees, their acceptance of the ways of the white settlers, and their willingness to fight alongside them. The civilization developed by the Cherokees is described.

Bishop, Robert, and Carter Houck. *All Flags Flying: The Great American Quilt Contest and Festival*. Dutton, 1986.

An insightful examination of a nineteenth-century social craft is provided in this book. Quilting is a genuine part of American cultural heritage.

Blassingame, Wyatt. *Jim Beckwourth: Black Trapper and Indian Chief*. Garrard, 1973.

This is the story of the famous mountain man, accepted by the Crows as war chief and by the whites as a great mountain man.

Blumberg, Rhoda. *The Incredible Journey of Lewis and Clark*. Lothrop, 1987.

The expedition led by Lewis and Clark to explore the unknown western regions of America at the beginning of the nineteenth century is described in this book.

Brown, Marion Marsh. *Sacagawea: Indian Interpreter to Lewis and Clark*. Children's Press, 1988.

This is a thoughtful, well-written biography of a remarkable Shoshone Indian woman.

Chambers, Catherine. *ADVENTURES IN FRONTIER AMERICA*. Troll, 1984.

Certain titles in this paperback series complement this unit and the unit on westward expansion (Section 5.7). Selected titles can be used for independent or cooperative assignments. This series is better suited for the classroom than the library.

D'Aulaire, Ingri, and Edgar P. D'Aulaire. *Abraham Lincoln*. Doubleday, 1987.

This biography of Lincoln is perhaps best noted for its narrative quality.

Fichter, George S. *First Steamboat Down the Mississippi*. Pelican Publishing Co., 1989.

A young boy is befriended by Nicholas Roosevelt, builder of the first steamboat, and joins him on its maiden voyage.

Josephy, Alvin M. *The Patriotic Chiefs: A Chronicle of American Indian Resistance*. Penguin, 1987.

The heroic and tragic history of Indian resistance to the white man from the seventeenth through the nineteenth centuries is told in terms of individuals who were there—Hiawatha, King Phillip, Pontiac, Tecumseh, Osceola, Black Hawk, Crazy Horse, and Chief Joseph.

Meadowcroft, Enid La Monte. *By Wagon and Flatboat*. Crowell, 1938.

In the period following the American Revolution, a time of growth and change, a family packs up its possessions and begins to move west to Ohio. The trip is filled with adventure.

Oppenheim, Joanne. *Osceola, Seminole Warrior*. Troll, 1979.

Oppenheim also offers other paperback booklets about Sequoyah, Tecumseh, and others. These booklets are better suited for classroom use than for library use.

Petersen, David, and Mark Coburn. *Meriwether Lewis and William Clark: Soldiers, Explorers, and Partners in History.* Children's Press, 1988.

Authentic pictures, diagrams, and diary excerpts are included in this account of the trailblazers.

Sloane, Eric. *Diary of an Early American Boy, Noah Blake, 1805.* Dodd, Mead, 1984.

Sloane's diagrams provide insight into everyday life, and the diary excerpts are authentic.

Smith, T. H. *Cry to the Night Wind.* Viking, 1986.

British Captain Spencer leads a survey team to North America and encounters storms, mutiny, and hostile Indians. The story of the captain's eleven-year-old son's capture and escape appeals to readers of this 1790s adventure story.

Spier, Peter. *The Erie Canal.* Doubleday, 1970.

This engaging, well-researched picture book is just right for discussing the canal and singing the well-known folk song.

Story of Transportation. Edited by Wilma Wilson Cain. Gateway Press, 1988.

This resource is usable in this unit for its discussion of flatboats, wagons, canal boats, and steamboats. Its chapters on clipper ships and sailing ships contain background information appropriate for Section 5.7.

Stoutenberg, Adrien. *American Tall Tales.* Penguin, 1976.

America's favorite tall tales are told in this collection: Paul Bunyan, Pecos Bill, John Henry, Stormalong, Mike Fink, Johnny Appleseed, Davy Crockett, and Joe Margarac.

Williams, Earl P. *What You Should Know About the American Flag.* Maryland Historical Press, 1987.

This paperbound work tells the history of the flag of the United States. Included are stories of the people and places connected with its design and use and information on how to display the flag properly.

5.7 The New Nation's Westward Expansion

Anderson, Joan. *Spanish Pioneers of the Southwest.* Lodestar, 1989.

Sharp black-and-white photographs in this book illustrate the hard life of these early settlers. The focus is on a New Mexico settlement where daily life of the mid-1700s is reenacted.

Brink, Carol Ryrie. *Caddie Woodlawn.* Macmillan, 1973.

This is the story of a spunky heroine on the Wisconsin frontier. Although the story is set in 1864, most of Caddie's experiences are typical of those of early pioneers.

The Diane Goode Book of American Folk Tales and Songs. Illustrated by Diane Goode; collected by Ann Dorell. Dutton, 1989.

A collection of traditional folk material, this book is usable throughout grade five.

Fisher, Leonard Everett. *The Oregon Trail.* Holiday, 1990.

The "main artery" of westward travel receives fine coverage, largely through the excellent primary sources included. See also Fisher's *The Alamo* (Holiday, 1987).

Freedman, Russell. *Indian Chiefs.* Holiday, 1987.

Six stories of western Indian chiefs who led their people during historic moments in U.S. history are offered by Freedman. See also *Buffalo Hunt* (Holiday, 1988) and *Cowboys of the Wild West* (Ticknor and Fields, 1985) by the same author.

Fritz, Jean. *Make Way for Sam Houston.* Putnam, 1986.

This is a compelling biography of the man who was truly one of the founding fathers of Texas.

Goble, Paul. *Death of the Iron Horse.* Bradbury, 1987.

The story of rail sabotage is told in this book from the Indians' point of view. In August, 1867, a group of young Cheyenne men tore up the rails and caused the wreck of a Union Pacific freight train.

Harvey, Brett. *My Prairie Year: Based on the Diary of Elenore Plaisted.* Holiday, 1986.

The life of nine-year-old Elenore Plaisted, who moved from Lincoln, Maine, to the vast prairies of the Dakota territory, is the subject of this book. Though set in 1889, this true story describes perils and pleasures typical of nineteenth-century prairie life.

Hill, William E. *The Oregon Trail, Yesterday and Today.* Caxton Printers, 1989.

Authentic photographs, sketches, and other primary source material are included in this teacher's resource. A detailed chronology is provided. See Hill's *California Trail* also.

Hilton, Suzanne. *Getting There: Frontier Travel Without Power.* Westminster Press, 1980.

Travel to the golden lands of the West was harrowing and difficult. The text is fascinating, and the book is well illustrated with old photographs and engravings. An index and bibliography are included.

Holling, Holling Clancy. *Tree in the Trail.* Houghton, 1970.

This distinguished picture book deals with change, continuity, and the Santa Fe Trail. Holling's *Paddle-to-the-Sea, Seabird,* and *Minn of the Mississippi* have the same format and complement other units.

Hotze, Sollace. *A Circle Unbroken.* Clarion, 1988.

In 1838, Rachel Porter is captured by the Sioux and brought up by the chief as his daughter until her father gets her back seven years later. This book was inspired by historical incidents.

Jakes, John. *Susanna of the Alamo: A True Story.* Illustrated by Paul Bacon. Harcourt, 1986.

A vivid retelling of the battle at the Alamo and the story of a brave young woman, Susanna Dickinson, who survived the massacre to bear witness, defied the powerful General Antonio López de Santa Anna, and inspired Sam Houston and his outnumbered band of Texans to defeat the Mexicans.

Levine, Ellen. *If You Travelled West in a Covered Wagon.* Scholastic, 1986.

The brief text of this book, presented in question-and-answer form, gives the reader an insight into the planning necessary for wagon travel and the kind of life experienced on a wagon train.

McGovern, Ann. *The Defenders.* Scholastic, 1987.

This book profiles three native American heroes—Osceola, Tecumseh, and Cochise, all great Indian leaders—and tells the story of their legendary fights for native Americans' rights.

MacLachlan, Patricia. *Sarah, Plain and Tall.* Harper, 1985.

This is the story of a mail-order bride who comes from Maine to make her home on the prairie.

O'Dell, Scott. *Sing Down the Moon.* Houghton, 1970.

The story of the "Long Walk," the forced 300-mile (482.7-kilometre) march of the Navajos from their canyon homes to Fort Sumner, is told in this book. The heroine of the story escapes with her future husband to return to their canyon and begin a new life.

Parkman, Francis. *The Oregon Trail.* Penguin, 1982.

This is a faithful record of life beyond the Mississippi River before the California gold rush began in 1849. Teachers should select excerpts.

Pelz, Ruth. *Black Heroes of the Wild West.* Open Hand Publishing, Inc., 1990.

Brief, vivid portraits of black heroes and heroines are rendered here. George Washington Bush, Clara Brown, and Bill Pickett are among the ten figures depicted.

Turner, Ann. *Grasshopper Summer.* Macmillan, 1989.

Though set in 1874, this novel depicts some of the aspects of homesteading common to earlier settlers, including sod houses, the vast expanses of land, and the destructive forces of nature.

Walker, Barbara. *The Little House Cookbook: Frontier Foods from Laura Ingalls Wilder's Classic Stories.* Harper, 1979.

The recipes in this book are based on the food pioneers ate on the way west. Quotes and descriptions from the *LITTLE HOUSE* books are included as well as a fine index, a bibliography, a glossary, and conversion tables.

West, Jessamyn. "Song of the Settlers," in *Favorite Poems Old and New.* Edited by Helen Ferris. Doubleday, 1957.

In a few stanzas, West captures the spirit and attitude of many nineteenth-century settlers.

Wilder, Laura Ingalls. *Little House on the Prairie.* Harper, 1953.

This is one of the eight titles that make up a notable group of American stories woven out of the author's vivid memories of her pioneer childhood. Though technically of a later period than 1850, the experiences Wilder presents were common to those of most pioneers.

5.8 Linking Past to Present: The American People, Then and Now

Adler, David. *Jackie Robinson: He Was the First.* Holiday, 1989.

This biography is easily read by most fifth graders. Robinson's hardships, tragedies, and triumphs are presented in a way that inspires admiration for this great athlete and citizen.

The American Reader, Words That Moved a Nation. Edited by Diane Ravitch. Harper Collins, 1990.

An extraordinary collection of essays, speeches, songs, and poems, this treasury contains writings by Americans about life in America from the time of the Mayflower Compact to the present day. The collection brings together under one cover the culturally diverse strands of U.S. society. Annotations help readers better appreciate the historical background and impact of over 200 writings. Schools should make every effort to have at least one copy as a resource for teachers of fifth grade students.

Ammon, Richard. *Growing Up Amish.* Atheneum, 1989.

With photographs, this autobiographical account is a valuable picture of an enduring culture in Pennsylvania. Marcia Adams's *Cooking from Quilt Country: Hearty Recipes from Amish and Mennonite Kitchens* (Potter, 1989) is a good foil for this book.

Beatty, Patricia. *Wait for Me, Watch for Me, Eula Bea.* Morrow, 1978.

Of the seven Collier family members, only three-year-old Eula Bea and her brother Lewtie remain after two have left to fight the Confederates and the rest have been killed by Comanches. The setting is Texas in 1861.

Bernsteom, Joanne E. *Dmitry: A Young Soviet Immigrant.* Houghton, 1981.

This is the story of Dmitry and his parents, recent immigrants to the United States from the Soviet Union, who found their first year in America more difficult than they had dreamed possible.

Branson, Karen. *Streets of Gold.* Putnam, 1981.

Fourteen-year-old Maureen O'Connor, her father, and two brothers journey from Ireland to America via steerage in 1847 during the potato famine.

Clark, Ann. *To Stand Against the Wind.* Viking, 1978.

A work of beauty and breadth, this book allows younger readers to empathize with a South Vietnamese family whose members' lives are disrupted by war.

Eger, Jeffrey. *The Statue in the Harbor: A Story of Two Apprentices.* Silver, Burdett, 1985.

This is the fictionalized account of a ten-year-old boy who is an apprentice in the Parisian foundry where the Statue of Liberty is being constructed. Information on the construction, installation, and celebration of one of the United States's greatest symbols is provided in this book.

Ferris, Jeri. *Arctic Explorer: The Story of Matthew Henson.* Carolrhoda, 1989.

This is the story of a remarkable black American, "the most nearly indispensable man" to Robert E. Peary. See also Ferris's *Space Challenger: The Story of Guion Bluford.*

Fisher, Aileen. "The Mother of Thanksgiving," in *Holiday Programs for Boys and Girls.* Plays, Inc., 1986.

This radio script tells of the achievements of nineteenth-century magazine editor Sara Josepha Hale. Her story demonstrates not only American values but also the effects of a private citizen's dogged determination. The script is easily adapted for a reader's theater.

Fisher, Leonard. *Across the Sea from Galway.* Four Winds, 1975.

The year is 1849. There is famine in Ireland, and children are being sent by their parents to Boston.

This is a story of survival, the love of family, and the unconquerable human spirit.

Freedman, Russell. *Immigrant Kids.* Dutton, 1980.

Photographs of the children of poor European immigrants to America 100 years ago are featured in this book. The children are shown attending school, working at various jobs, and playing. Photos of life in immigration ships are included.

Hamilton, Virginia. *The Bells of Christmas.* Harcourt, 1989.

This portrait of a midwestern black family's 1890 celebration helps students understand a way of life prior to the age of the automobile.

Hancock, Sibyl. *Famous Firsts of Black Americans.* Pelican Publishing Co., 1983.

This book consists of brief biographical sketches of such notables as Phillis Wheatley, Charles Richard Drew, and Richard Allen.

Hicks, Josephus, and Ellen Hicks. *Black Image Makers.* New Day Press, 1988.

This paperbound teacher's resource contains portraits of noteworthy black Americans. Illustrations by students are featured.

Hoyt-Goldsmith, Diane. *Totem Pole.* Holiday, 1990.

This book contains the old Tsimshian tale "The Legend of the Eagle and the Young Chief." Color photographs of contemporary American Indian life and accompanying text show continuity through tradition.

Hughes, Langston, and Arna Bontemps. *The Book of Negro Folklore.* Dodd, Mead, 1983.

This valuable compendium of black American heritage can be used by both teachers and students.

Jacobs, William Jay. *Ellis Island: New Hope in a New Land.* Scribner, 1990.

Authentic black-and-white photographs illustrate this easy-to-read account of this famous entry point to America.

Kherdian, David. *A Song for Uncle Harry.* Philomel, 1989.

Armenian-American life is reflected in this affectionate story set in the Midwest during the Great Depression. In its depiction of diversity in U.S. life, the book addresses learnings in the framework's National Identity strand.

Lazarus, Emma. "The New Colossus," in *Favorite Poems Old and New.* Edited by Helen Ferris. Doubleday, 1957.

This poem ("Give me your tired, your poor. . .") is engraved at the base of the Statue of Liberty.

Lenski, Lois. *Strawberry Girl.* Lippincott, 1988.

This and other regional stories Lenski wrote years ago reflect part of our history; they provide one more glimpse of the diversity in our national identity. See also *Prairie School* (Harper, 1951) by the same author.

Levitin, Sonia. *Journey to America.* Macmillan, 1986.

This story of a young Jewish girl who comes to America from Adolph Hitler's Germany to meet her father offers a picture of the world being turned upside down. How people show kindness or cruelty to the refugees is part of the story.

Lord, Bette Bao. *In the Year of the Boar and Jackie Robinson.* Harper, 1984.

Shirley Temple Wong comes to America from China in 1947, speaking no English. She must adjust as a fifth grader amidst American culture in Brooklyn. This is a deservedly popular novel.

McKissack, Patricia. *Mary McLeod Bethune: A Great American Educator.* Children's Press, 1985.

This is the biography of Mary McLeod Bethune, who made numerous contributions to education and advised several presidents. The PEOPLE OF DISTINCTION biographical series also contains worthwhile books about Frederick Douglass and Paul Laurence Dunbar.

Moore, Clement Clarke. *The Night Before Christmas; Or, A Visit from St. Nicholas.* Philomel Books, 1989.

This book offers a faithful reproduction of an 1870 publication. The classic poem is one example of how immigrants influenced the development of American culture. Moore's St. Nick was a combination of the European "Father Christmas" and an old Dutch caretaker Moore knew in his youth. Fifth graders can consider how traditions from older countries continue to influence current traditions and practices in the United States.

Moskin, Marietta. *Waiting for Mama.* Coward, 1975.

Becky was left in Russia with a sick baby when the rest of the family emigrated to the United States. Many abrupt changes in a short life create a dramatic true-to-life story.

Nhuong, Huynh Quang. *The Land I Lost.* Harper, 1986.

This autobiography of a boy born and raised in a small village in Vietnam includes stories of the family, the family's neighbors—both people and animals—and a pet water buffalo.

O'Connor, Jim. *Jackie Robinson and the Story of All-Black Baseball.* Random, 1989.

The great Brooklyn Dodger serves as an inspiration to all students in the United States, regardless of their ethnic backgrounds. The text is simple to read and may be usable in third grade as well.

Sachs, Marilyn. *Call Me Ruth.* Doubleday, 1982.

In the early 1900s, Rifka and her mother, Faigel, emigrate from Russia to the United States to join father. Personal and cultural hardships are described in this book.

Shapiro, Mary J. *How They Built the Statue of Liberty.* Random, 1985.

Mary Shapiro's in-depth discussion is based in large part on conversations with members of the statue's restoration team. The book is enhanced by beautiful black-and-white sketches that are based on old photographs and diagrams.

Siebert, Diane, and Wendell Minor. *Heartland.* Crowell, 1989.

Heartland, U.S.A., is impressively depicted here in verse and picture.

Sterne, Emma Gelders. *The Slave Ship.* Scholastic, 1983 (original title: *The Long Black Schooner*).

Kidnapped from their homes in West Africa and held in chains aboard a ship, the slaves find themselves in the middle of a strange ocean, miles from home. On the night of June 30, 1839, a young slave cuts his chains and tries to free the others.

Talbot, Charlene. *An Orphan for Nebraska.* Atheneum, 1979.

Eleven-year-old Kevin O'Rourke comes to New York in 1872. This slice of American historical fiction depicts western migration, the Children's Aid Society, New York street scenes, and the frontier.

Walter, Mildred Pitts. *Justin and the Best Biscuits in the World.* Lothrop, 1986.

Warm family values permeate this story of Justin's struggle to grow up and forget about "women's work." The story weaves westward migration, black cowboys, Bill Pickett, Nate Love, and "exodusters" into a theme of personal heritage in contemporary life. See also *Have a Happy . . .* (Lothrop, 1989) by the same author.

What a Morning! The Christmas Story in Black Spirituals. Edited by John Langstaff. Margaret K. McElderry Books, 1987.

This is a collection of black spirituals with spectacular illustrations by Ashley Bryan.

Yates, Elizabeth. *Amos Fortune, Free Man.* Dutton, 1967.

Amos Fortune, brought in slavery from Africa, was first owned by a Quaker and later by a tanner who taught him his trade and allowed him to buy his freedom.

Grade Six:
World History
and Geography—
Ancient Civilizations

6.1 Early Humankind and the Development of Human Societies

Anderson, Margaret. *Light in the Mountain*. Knopf, 1982.

Existence in a cold and harsh climate created challenges the early Maori people had to overcome.

Baumann, H. *Las Cuevas de los Grandes Cazadores*. Barcelona: Juventud, n.d.

This Spanish-language book discusses cave life and the hunters of early times.

Branigan, Keith. *Prehistory*. Watts, 1986.

The food, technology, society, and religion of prehistoric peoples are reconstructed and examined in this work through evidence from various archaeological sites.

Caselli, Giovanni. *The First Civilizations*. Bedrick, 1985.

The development of material, culture, and technology from the earliest toolmakers four million years ago to the Greeks 2,400 years ago is the subject of this book.

Caselli, Giovanni. *Las Primeras Civilizaciones*. Madrid: Generales Anaya, 1985 (Colección La Vida en el Pasado).

A usable resource on early civilization, this Spanish-language book is best suited for advanced readers.

Davidson, Marshall. *A History of Art from 25,000 B.C. to the Present*. Random, 1984.

A historical and cultural overview of art from prehistoric times through modern eras is presented in this book.

Denzel, Justin. *The Boy of the Painted Cave*. Philomel Books, 1988.

A boy is banished from his clan for breaking a taboo. This book presents a good picture of the social order of clans.

Dunrea, Olivier. *Skara Brae: The Story of a Prehistoric Village*. Holiday, 1986.

A detailed account is given in this book of the history of a 4,000-year-old archaeological site on the Orkney Islands. The text and extensive black-and-white drawings portray life in the Neolithic "village of hilly dunes." Excavation efforts are described.

Dyer, T. A. *A Way of His Own*. Houghton, 1981.

A lame boy from a very primitive nomadic tribe is abandoned by his family and together with a girl stolen from another tribe tries to survive a cruel winter.

Garcia, Ann O'Neal. *Spirit on the Wall*. Holiday, 1982.

The fiercely independent Mat-Maw, who lives in the inner depths of a cave, defies all her clan's customs to develop her granddaughter's artistic gift.

El Hombre Prehistórico. México: Los Grandes Libros, 1985.

Prehistoric humankind is the topic of this book, which is written in Spanish and recommended for better readers.

Lebrun, Francoise. *The Days of the Cave People*. Translated by Christopher Sharp. Silver Burdett, 1986.

In this story, a young cave dweller hunts and fishes with the men of his tribe and observes how tools are made. Information on prehistoric life is woven into the fabric of the story.

Mundy, Simon. *The Usborne Story of Music*. Hayes Books (EDC Publishing), 1980.

Though not literature, some students initially find the Usborne history series a good research resource because of its format. The series should be used discriminately. This book is usable throughout the sixth and seventh grades, too. See also Peppin's *Story of Painting* (EDC, 1980).

Pryor, Bonnie. *Seth of the Lion People*. Morrow, 1988.

Seth, an orphan boy with a withered leg, leaves his cave clan and makes his home with the Goat People. This book presents a portrait of our prehistoric past.

Seymour, Peter. *Discovering Our Past.* Macmillan, 1987.

> Archaeologists have discovered clues that help us recreate and learn about past civilizations.

Steele, William. *The Magic Amulet.* Harcourt, 1979.

> During prehistoric times, Tragg's family clan abandons him because his wounded leg slows their hunting and gathering. Watching an armadillo defend itself from a wolf inspires him to fend for himself.

Sutcliff, Rosemary. *Warrior Scarlet.* Oxford, 1958.

> In this story set in the Bronze Age, Drem anticipates the day when he will become a warrior and be able to wear the scarlet cloak signifying manhood in his tribe. Drem, however, has only one good arm, and his grandfather believes that Drem will never be able to become a warrior. Drem sets out to prove him wrong.

Turnbull, Ann. *Maroo of the Winter Caves.* Clarion, 1984.

> In the last Ice Age in the south of France, Maroo, a teenage girl, must save her family from the on-slaught of the icy winter.

Turner, Ann. *Time of the Bison.* Macmillan, 1987.

> Scar Boy, a young cave dweller, seeks identity and the useful application of his gifts in this short, readable work of historical fiction.

Wibberley, Leonard. *Attar of the Ice Valley.* Farrar, 1968.

> Attar, a young hunter in approximately 50,000 B.C., lives with his small tribe in an area completely covered with ice.

6.2   Beginnings of Civilization in the Near East and Africa: Mesopotamia, Egypt, and Kush

El Antiguo Egipto. Spain: Altea (Colección Benjamín Información), n.d.

> This book in Spanish on ancient Egypt has a companion volume about ancient Rome.

Asimov, Isaac. *The Egyptians.* Houghton, 1967.

> The writer offers a complete survey of Egyptian history from the origins of farming through the dynasties to today's world.

Bryson, Bernarda. *Gilgamesh: Man's First Story.* Holt, 1966.

> This is a version of the oldest legend known to humankind. First written in Sumerian cuneiform 3,000 years before the birth of Christ, this stirring epic contains the seeds of the great mythological heroes Hercules, Jason, and Theseus.

Carter, Dorothy. *His Majesty, Queen Hatshepsut.* Lippincott, 1987.

> A fictionalized account of the life of Hatshepsut, a queen in ancient Egypt who declared herself pharaoh and ruled as such for more than 20 years, is given in this book.

Cleopatra. Editora Cinco (Líderes del Mundo), n.d.

> Translated into Spanish from the Chelsea House title of the same name, this biography touches on culture and history during the reign of Egypt's famous queen.

Coblence, Jean-Michel. *The Earliest Cities.* Silver Burdett, 1987.

> This volume, one of the *Human Story* series, contains useful information regarding Mesopotamia and Sumer, but certain chapters also deal with archaeologists and complement Section 6.1.

Cribb, Joe. *Eyewitness Books: Money.* Knopf, 1990.

> Color photographs of historic monies are this book's most outstanding feature. This work may be used in more than one unit but is listed here because of its pictures of Mesopotamian currency.

Dioses y Faraones de la Mitología Egipcia. Madrid: Generales Anaya, 1986.

> Intended for somewhat advanced readers, this book discusses gods and pharaohs of early Egypt. It is written in Spanish.

Duche, Jean. *The Great Trade Routes.* McGraw-Hill, 1973.

> Richly illustrated, this well-written and most informative book traces the beginnings of trade from the

Neolithic village dwellers through the age of exploration up to contemporary times.

English, Raymond, et al. CONCEPTS AND INQUIRY: THE HUMAN ADVENTURE series (Second edition only—multiple volumes). Educational Research Council of America, Allyn and Bacon, 1975.

Good visuals and simple narration pervade this old textbook series, and geography and history are well integrated. The *Ancient Civilization* volume is pertinent to this unit; *Greek and Roman Civilization* and *Four World Views* are usable volumes in later units. Out of print, this series can be used as a teacher's resource.

Gardner, John, and John Maier. *Gilgamesh*. Knopf, 1984.

The Gilgamesh historical epic is presented in this book. See also Herbert Mason's translation (New American Library paperback, 1972). Excerpts of this work may be presented as choral reading or for a readers' theater.

Glubok, Shirley. *The Art of Ancient Egypt*. Atheneum, 1962.

People who lived in Egypt 5,000 years ago come alive in this book about wall paintings, scrolls, statues, gods, sailboats, mirrors, toys, and games. See also *The Art of Egypt Under the Pharaohs*.

Green, Roger. *Tales of Ancient Egypt*. Penguin Puffin, 1972.

This is a concise collection of the myths, folktales, and legends of ancient Egypt. Possibly suitable also for younger readers, this work is still usable.

Hackwell, W. John. *Signs, Letters, Words: Archaeology Discovers Writing*. Scribner, 1987.

Ancient humans had speech, but memory was the only means to store accumulated knowledge. As changes took place in societies, the development of writing was a natural outgrowth.

Harris, Geraldine. *Gods and Pharaohs from Egyptian Mythology*. Schocken Press, 1983.

This helpful resource depicts ancient Egypt's religion, government, and culture.

Hart, George. *Exploring the Past: Ancient Egypt*. Harcourt, 1989.

Features of public and private life are presented with accuracy and visual appeal in this book.

Ions, Veronica. *Egyptian Mythology*. Bedrick, 1983. Egyptian myths make up this collection.

Kinder, Herman, and Werner Hilgemann. *Anchor Atlas of World History* (Vol. I and II). Doubleday, 1978.

This book is a valuable resource for teachers of ancient history.

Kramer, Samuel N. *History Begins at Sumer: Thirty-Nine "Firsts" in Man's Recorded History*. University of Pennsylvania Press, 1981.

A fascinating and surprising account of this ancient civilization's innovations is contained in this book.

Lauber, Patricia. *Tales Mummies Tell*. Harper, 1985.

This book explains how the study of mummies can reveal information about ancient civilizations and prehistoric life. See also Aliki's *Mummies Made in Egypt*.

Macaulay, David. *Pyramid*. Houghton, 1975.

Exquisite black-and-white drawings, accompanied by succinct text, demonstrate the step-by-step process of building an Egyptian pyramid.

McDermott, Gerald. *The Voyage of Osiris: A Myth of Ancient Egypt*. Windmill, 1977.

With little text and excellent color illustrations, this book retells an Egyptian myth of over 5,000 years ago.

McGraw, Eloise. *Mara, Daughter of the Nile*. Penguin, 1985.

Mara is a seventeen-year-old Egyptian slave girl living during the reign of Hatshepsut around 1550 B.C. See also *The Golden Goblet* (Penguin, 1986) by the same author.

Manniche, Lise. *The Prince Who Knew His Fate*. Putnam, 1982.

An ancient story, accompanied by a translation of the hieroglyphics that stretch along the bottoms of the pages, carries the reader deep into Egyptian culture and customs.

Moss, Carol. *Science in Ancient Mesopotamia*. Watts, 1988.

Libraries will also want to consider companion volumes pertaining to Greece and Rome.

Nesbit, E. *The Story of the Amulet.* Dell (Yearling Classics), 1987.

An amulet allows a group of youngsters to go back in time and visit different historical periods and places, ancient Egypt among them. This mixture of fantasy with historical fiction is a classic that is usable in other units as well.

Neurath, Marie. *They Lived Like This in Ancient Mesopotamia.* Watts, 1964.

A brief discussion of life in ancient Mesopotamia that includes geography, housing, and communication is contained in this book.

Odijk, Pamela. *The Egyptians.* Silver Burdett, 1990.

This newly published book contains general information on ancient Egyptian culture. Sixth graders will find the format attractive.

Oliphant, Margaret. *The Egyptian World.* Warwick, 1989.

History, archaeology, culture, and society are presented in a clear, attractive format in this book that includes a discussion of the New Kingdom.

Payne, Elizabeth. *The Pharaohs of Ancient Egypt.* Random, 1981.

This *LANDMARK* series paperback is valuable reading for teachers as well as students. A treatment of history, anthropology, and culture is included.

Perl, Lila. *Mummies, Tombs, and Treasure: Secrets of Ancient Egypt.* Clarion, 1987.

Lila Perl's fascinating and thorough account of the Egyptian way of death will be certain to fire the imaginations of readers of all ages.

Readings in Ancient History: Thought and Experience from Gilgamesh to St. Augustine. Edited by Nels Bailkey. Heath, 1987.

This is a valuable teacher's resource that contains primary source material. It includes Hebrew writings, the apology of Socrates, the Melian Dialogue, writings of Cicero, and other material.

Robinson, Charles Alexander. *The First Book of Ancient Mesopotamia and Persia.* Watts, 1962.

This book takes a look at the Sumerian, Babylonian, and Assyrian civilizations.

Roux, Georges. *Ancient Iraq* (Revised edition). Penguin, 1976.

This teacher's resource presents a history of the rise and fall of great Mesopotamian empires from Sumer through Parthia.

Sethus, Michel. *The Days of the Pharaohs.* Translated by Christopher Sharp. Silver Burdett, 1986.

The daily activities of a family in ancient Egypt are followed in this book. Information on dress, houses, religious rites, legends, and games is given in a simplified text and in clear, colorful illustrations.

Sheppard, E. J. *Ancient Egypt.* Longman, 1960.

The history, rulers, and culture of ancient Egypt are discussed in this book.

Stolz, Mary. *Cat in the Mirror.* Dell, 1978.

Two girls living 3,000 years apart—one in present-day New York and the other in ancient Egypt—become aware of each other's existence. See also *Zekmet, the Stone Carver* (Harcourt, 1987) by the same author.

"The Sun-God and the Dragon," in *In the Beginning: Creation Stories from Around the World.* Retold by Virginia Hamilton. Harcourt, 1988.

This myth of Ra, the creator, was recorded on papyrus dating from 300 B.C. but is said to be of earlier origin. See also "Marduk, God of Gods" in the same collection.

El Tiempo de los Faraones. Lyon, Spain: Everest (Colección Saber Más), n.d.

The culture, history, archaeology, and geography of Egyptian civilization are featured in this Spanish-language book. Illustrations, maps, and photos are included.

Unstead, R. J. *See Inside an Egyptian Town.* Warwick, 1978.

The buildings and activities in an Egyptian town begun in 1375 B.C. are discussed in this book.

Van Loon, Hendrik. *The Story of Mankind.* Liveright, 1985.

Van Loon has his prejudices and controversies, but he is able to connect ancient history to the present day. Excerpts from this book are usable in other units and other grades.

Ventura, Piero. *There Once Was a Time.* Putnam, 1987.

Concentrating on the ordinary people of eight significant periods of Western civilization, an artist shows within each era nine aspects of life: society, homes, agriculture, crafts, trade, dress, transportation, inventions, and warfare. This book can be used era by era or to follow the thread of development through history.

Weisgard, Leonard. *The Beginning of Cities: The Recreating in Pictures and Text of Mesopotamian Life from Farming to Early City Building.* Coward, 1968.

A study of the changes that took place in the New Stone Age after the development of farming when communities began to gather in the fertile Tigris-Euphrates Valley.

Woods, Geraldine. *Science in Ancient Egypt.* Watts, 1988.

This is an excellent resource for this unit. See also George Beshore's *Science in Ancient China* (Watts, 1988).

6.3   The Foundation of Western Ideas: The Ancient Hebrews and Greeks

Asimov, Isaac. *The Greeks: A Great Adventure.* Houghton, 1965.

Asimov traces the history of the Greek civilization, which began more than 4,000 years ago and whose influence in culture, politics, and philosophy encompassed half the world. See also Asimov's *Words from the Myths* (Signet, 1969).

Barbieri, G. *Vida Cotidiana en la Grecia de Pericles.* Spain: Avance (Enciclopedia Monográfica Avance), n.d.

This Spanish-language book focuses on daily life in the time of Pericles.

Barth, Edna. *Cupid and Psyche: A Love Story.* Clarion, 1976.

The Greek god of love, Cupid, falls in love with the beautiful mortal Psyche in this book. See also *The Arrow and the Lamp* by Margaret Hodges (1989).

The Bible. Various versions.

Genesis and other books in the Bible contain the account of creation, the universal flood, Hebrew history, and poetry.

La Biblia para Niños. Spain: Nebrija, 1981.

These Spanish-language Bible stories for children may be used in this and in later units.

Chaikin, Miriam. *Ask Another Question: The Story and Meaning of Passover.* Clarion, 1986.

A teacher's or student's resource that explains events given in the biblical book of Exodus, this book is usable at more than one grade level.

Cohen, Barbara. *I Am Joseph.* Lothrop, 1980.

A vivid retelling of the story of Joseph, relating how he was sold into slavery, taken to Egypt, and eventually reunited with his family.

Colum, Padraic. *The Golden Fleece: And the Heroes Who Lived Before Achilles.* Macmillan, 1982.

The adventures of Jason, who sought the Golden Fleece, are interwoven in this book with other myths and hero stories about Orpheus, Pandora, Atlanta, Peleus, and Theseus. See also *The Children's Homer: The Adventures of Odysseus and the Tale of Troy* (Macmillan, 1982) by the same author.

Coolidge, Olivia. *Marathon Looks on the Sea.* Houghton, 1967.

Metiachos, the son of Greek General Miltiades, leads his Persian soldiers to the Battle of Marathon, where the Greeks triumph. See also *Hercules and Other Tales from Greek Myths* (Scholastic, 1961).

D'Aulaire, Ingri, and Edgar D'Aulaire. *D'Aulaire's Book of Greek Myths.* Doubleday, 1980.

This book offers a brief retelling of Greek myths with full-color pictures.

de la Mare, Walter. *Stories from the Bible: From the Garden of Eden to the Promised Land.* Faber and Faber, 1987.

This book contains 34 stories retold from the Hebrew Bible.

Dia, E. *Pericles*. Spain: Araluce (Grandes Hombres), n.d.

Greece's great ruler could show traits of enlightened leadership, and this is his biography. It is most appropriate for advanced Spanish readers.

En el Tiempo de los Hebreos. Leon, Spain: Everest (Colección Saber Más).

Illustrations, maps, and photographs accompany this Spanish-language discussion of the ancient Hebrews.

Exodus. Adapted by Mirian Chaikin. Holiday, 1987.

This is a sophisticated picture book with a dignified retelling of the Israelites' departure from Egyptian bondage and their ultimate arrival in the land of Canaan. A map of the probable route of the Exodus is provided, as well as the symbols of the 12 tribes.

Fisher, Leonard Everett. *Jason and the Golden Fleece*. Holiday, 1990.

With this dramatic picture book, Fisher adds another retelling to his other works, *The Olympians* and *Theseus and the Minotaur*. These books are attractive fare for sixth graders. His *The Wailing Wall* complements this unit in its relationship to the ancient Hebrews.

Gates, Doris. *A Fair Wind for Troy*. Illustrated by Charles Mikolaycak. Penguin, 1984.

One of a series of retellings of Greek myths, this title deals with the abduction of Helen and ends with the great Trojan horse and the death of Agamemnon. See also *The Golden God: Apollo; Lord of the Sky: Zeus; Two Queens of Heaven: Aphrodite and Demeter;* and *The Warrior Goddess: Athena*, all by the same author.

Geisert, Arthur. *The Ark*. Houghton, 1988.

Detailed, etched illustrations and simple text mark these interpretations of the biblical story of Noah and the ark. Many cutaways of the ark's interior are included.

Glubok, Shirley, and Alfred Tamarin. *Olympic Games in Ancient Greece*. Harper, 1976.

This is an account of the games at the height of their glory. Their history is the history of Greece. A rich panorama of Greek life, history, and culture is provided in this book.

Goldreich, Gloria. *A Treasury of Jewish Literature: From Biblical Times to Today*. Holt, 1982.

This book is a compendium of great Jewish writings ranging from the Bible to the works of Philip Roth. Selected examples include the Talmud, the Zahar, the tales of Sholom Aleichem, and the work of Nobel Laureate S. Y. Agnon. A brief introduction provides historical background to this teacher's resource.

Gottlieb, Gerald. *The Adventures of Ulysses*. Linnett Books, 1988.

This is a novel-length treatment of the saga of Ulysses. Gottlieb presents the legend chronologically and as an adventure story.

Green, Roger Lancelyn. *Tale of Troy*. Penguin, 1974.

In addition to this retelling, see also Green's *Tales of Greek Heroes*.

Harris, Nathaniel. *Alexander the Great and the Greeks*. Watts, 1986.

This story begins in 1900 B.C. and carries the reader through the victories and defeats of the Greek people.

Hawthorne, Nathaniel. *Tanglewood Tales*. Ohio State University Press, 1981.

This and *A Wonder Book* (available together in one volume) contain Hawthorne's adaptations of ancient myths. Classes might compare his retellings with those of other retellers. Hawthorne is perhaps best introduced in this way, years before students read *The Scarlet Letter* or his short stories.

Herrera, Juan Ignacio. *Alejandro Magno*. Spain: Susaeta, 1981.

This biography in Spanish of Alexander the Great is best suited for readers at this grade level and above.

Hewitt, Kathryn. *King Midas and the Golden Touch*. Harcourt, 1987.

In this retelling of Nathaniel Hawthorne's classic, a king who wishes for the golden touch is faced with its consequences when his wish is granted.

Household, Geoffrey. *The Exploits of Xenophon.* Linnet Books, 1989.

Originally published by Random House as a Landmark book, this reprint offers a retelling of the Greek military leader's memoirs.

Ipsen, D. C. *Archimedes: Greatest Scientist of the Ancient World.* Enslow, 1988.

Sun rays, the block and tackle, and the value of *pi* are just a few of the important discoveries of the Syracuse scientist. The book is noted for honesty, accuracy, and readability.

Keller, Werner. *The Bible as History.* Bantam, 1974.

This book is possibly best used as a teacher's resource. It is also usable as part of the unit included in Section 6.5. A book better suited for students is Keller's *Bible as History Through Pictures* (Thames and Hudson, 1964), a book that deserves republication for its pictorial emphasis.

Kingsley, Charles. *The Heroes.* Smith, 1980.

The splendid retellings by this nineteenth-century English author are probably too difficult for some sixth graders to read. Students should, however, hear them read well.

Kuskin, Karla. *Jerusalem, Shining Still.* Harper, 1987.

This book's lilting, poetic prose and glowing, golden woodcuts tell the 4,000-year history of Jerusalem. It is an elegant and stirring homage to this holy city.

Lasker, Joe. *The Greek Alexander the Great.* Viking, 1983.

The life of the warrior king of Macedonia who conquered and unified the known world is traced in this book.

Lewis, Naomi. *Cry Wolf and Other Aesop Fables.* Oxford, 1988.

A stunning but maverick treatment of the fables is presented in this book. For a more traditional collection, see James Reeves's *Fables from Aesop* (Bedrick, 1985).

Ling, Roger. *The Greek World.* Bedrick, 1988.

This author traces the history of the classical Greek world as it has been revealed through archaeology and the work of antiquarians. A complete picture from literature to politics is presented.

Low, Alice. *The Macmillan Book of Greek Gods and Heroes.* Macmillan, 1985.

Tales of gods and humans struggling with life's dilemmas are presented in this well-illustrated volume of Greek myths. The flavor of the 33 original stories is retained in this collection.

McDermott, Gerald. *Sun Flight.* Four Winds, 1980.

In this artful retelling of the Icarus and Daedalus legend, the climax of the story is told entirely through pictures. This title is out of print.

McEvedy, Colin. *The Penguin Atlas of Ancient History.* Penguin, 1986.

Historical atlases are frequently helpful as background for teachers and as a students' reference. This one is handy and inexpensive.

McLean, Mollie, and Anne Wiseman. *Adventures of the Greek Heroes.* Houghton, 1972.

Noteworthy for its simple, faithful retellings of Greek epics, this book is an excellent selection for less able readers.

Martelli, Stelio. *Iliada: La Guerra de Troya. Odisea: Aventuras de Ulises.* Madrid: Edaf, 1984.

Homer's *Iliad* and *The Odyssey* are offered in Spanish.

La Odisea. Raintree Classics, 1981.

An adaptation of Homer's *The Odyssey* is presented here for Spanish readers.

Osborne, Mary Pope. *Favorite Greek Myths.* Scholastic, 1989.

The myths in this attractive collection are engagingly narrated.

Petersham, Maud. *David.* Barcelona: Juventud, n.d.

A companion volume to this Spanish work is *Moisés* (Moses) from the same publisher.

Powell, Anton. *The Greek World.* Warwick Press, 1987.

This beautifully illustrated book describing the events in Greek history from 1500 to 400 B.C. can be used as a teacher's resource along with *The Legend of Odysseus,* by Peter Connolly (Oxford, 1986).

Purdy, Susan. *Ancient Greece.* Watts, 1982.

This book briefly describes ancient Greek civilization and gives instructions for making various Greek artifacts.

Russell, William F. *Classic Myths to Read Aloud: The Classic Stories of Greek and Roman Mythology Specially Arranged by an Education Consultant.* Crown, 1989.

This is a compendium of Greek and Roman myths retold by a noted reteller. See also Russell's *Classics to Read Aloud to Your Children* (Crown, 1984).

Schwartz, Lynne. *The Four Questions.* Dial, 1989.

Passover is explained and illustrated here in a way that links ancient times to the present. The four questions of the seder are a feature of this book.

Simon, Norma. *Passover.* Crowell, 1965.

An account of the Jews' suffering under the pharaohs and their flight from Egypt is provided in this book.

Switzer, Ellen, and Costas Switzer. *Greek Myths: Gods, Heroes and Monsters—Their Sources, Their Stories and Their Meanings.* Atheneum, 1988.

These authors acquaint readers with the Greek pantheon from Zeus to Pan and tell stories of Hercules, Jason, Peleus, and Antigone.

Theseus and the Minotaur. Retold by Warwick Hutton. McElderry, 1989.

A simple, evocative retelling of the myth in picture-book form.

Walsh, Jill Paton. *Crossing to Salamis.* Heinemann, 1977.

This book tells of Aster's journey from Athens in 497 B.C., with her mother, servant, and friend, to Salamis as Persians under Xerxes invade the city.

Woodford, Susan. *The Parthenon.* Lerner, 1983.

An account is provided of the design, building, decoration, and eventual destruction of the temple dedicated to Athena. Aspects of Greek life and worship are explained.

6.4　West Meets East: The Early Civilizations of India and China

Adam, Daisy. *Poems from India.* Crowell, 1970.

Adam's collection contains a wide variety of poems that are representative of the many cultures, languages, traditions, and time frames of India. The quality of the translation and the selections has been noted by reviewers. This book is out of print.

Bahree, Patricia. *The Hindu World.* Silver Burdett, 1983.

All aspects of Hindu society are treated in this brief but comprehensive look at a very rich heritage.

Bancroft, Anne. *The Buddhist World.* Silver Burdett, 1985.

With the use of vivid photographs, maps, and drawings, the history of Buddhism is traced from its beginnings in India to its spread throughout most of Asia.

Buck, Pearl. *Fairy Tales of the Orient.* Simon and Schuster, 1965.

Buck has collected 36 fairy tales and folktales from China, Japan, India, and other parts of the Orient. Her book is now out of print.

Confucius. *The Wisdom of Confucius.* American Classical College Press, 1982.

This is a handy compendium of sayings by the great Chinese philosopher and teacher.

Daly, Bridget. *Gopal and the Temple's Secret: My Village in India.* Silver Burdett, 1985.

A complex culture with a multitude of customs is experienced in this book through the daily life of a ten-year-old boy living in a small village.

De Roin, Nancy. *Jataka Tales.* Houghton Mifflin, 1975.

These stories, based on Buddha's teachings, are from India and are traced back over centuries. This book deserves republication.

Dragones, Dioses y Espíritus de la Mitología China. Madrid: Generales Anaya, n.d.

Chinese mythology is discussed in this book, which is suitable for Spanish-speaking students of slightly advanced reading ability.

Dutton, Maude. *The Tortoise and the Geese and Other Fables of the Bidpai.* Houghton, 1935.

E. Boyd Smith's illustrations grace this classic collection of philosophical tales from Kashmir. This book deserves republication.

Fisher, Leonard Everett. *The Great Wall of China.* Macmillan, 1986.

This is a graphic telling of the political climate of the time and the epic feat that was the building of the Great Wall approximately 2,200 years ago. A map, a subsequent history of the Great Wall, and a translation of several Chinese characters are included.

Galbraith, Catherine. *India, Now and Through Time.* Houghton, 1980.

This book introduces the land, history, culture, and people of India from the year 1500 B.C. to the present.

Glubok, Shirley. *The Art of China.* Macmillan, 1973.

The history and cultural background of Chinese art are traced in this book from prehistoric times to the present.

Goff, Denise. *Early China.* Watts, 1986.

Chinese geography, the origins of the people, early agricultural methods, writing, religions, and technological advances are described in this book.

Gray, J. A. B. *East Indian Tales and Legends.* Oxford, 1989.

This paperback collection includes a wide range of ancient tales and fables. Also included is the *Ramayana.*

Hughes-Stanton, Penelope. *See Inside an Ancient Chinese Town.* Watts, 1986.

Photographs, reproductions of paintings, drawings, maps, and building layouts are combined in this book to show how life was really lived in ancient China. Interspersed among graphic elements are commentaries on religion and important personages.

Jaffrey, Madhur. *Seasons of Splendour: Tales, Myths, and Legends from India.* Atheneum, 1985.

This selection of stories, with vivid illustrations that recount some of the myths and legends of India, is arranged in the sequence in which the stories might have been told at religious festivals during the course of the Hindu lunar calendar year.

Kamen, Gloria. *The Ringdoves: From the Fables of Bidpai.* Atheneum, 1988.

This illustrated book is a retelling of an Indian fable.

Lattimore, Deborah Nourse. *The Dragon's Robe.* Harper, 1989.

The significance of the dragon in Chinese folklore is central to this story of a poor weaver's noble spirit. Lattimore's illustrations enhance the tale through her use of authentic Chinese symbols and artistic styles.

Lord, Bette Bao. *Spring Moon.* Avon, 1982.

This paperback novel depicts five generations in China and reflects the role of women in the culture.

Miller, Luree. *The Black Hat Dances: Two Buddhist Boys in the Himalayas.* Putnam, 1987.

Buddhism affects every aspect of the lives of two boys living in Sikkim, in the northeast corner of India. One child is a novice in a monastery, and the other lives on a small farm.

Mukerji, Dhan Gopol. *Gay-Neck: The Story of a Pigeon.* Dutton, 1968.

A reprint of an early Newberry Medal winner, this novel is set in twentieth-century Calcutta. Its inclusion here is based on the underlying values and interpretations of Buddhism that could indirectly complement the unit. The book is easy reading for sixth graders.

Nancarrow, Peter. *Early China and the Wall.* Lerner, 1980.

This short, compact history of early China traces the development of the Great Wall, the ruling style, and the social orders imposed by various rulers of China.

Ram, Govinder. *Rama and Sita: A Folk Tale from India.* Bedrick, 1988.

A tale from the *Ramayana* is illustrated in this book. Marcia Brown's *Once a Mouse* (Scribner, 1961) is taken from the *Hitopadesa* and can be a thought-provoking fable for this grade level.

Rowland-Entwistle, Tehadore. *Confucius and Ancient China.* Watts, 1987.

> The story and life of Confucius introduces students to the land of ancient China and its development from a collection of tribes to a unified state under the first emperor.

Sadler, Catherine. *Heaven's Reward: Fairy Tales from China.* Atheneum, 1985.

> A collection of six tales taken from traditional Chinese versions that are drawn from Confucian and Taoist philosophy.

Saunders, Tao. *Dragons, Gods and Spirits from Chinese Mythology.* Schocken, 1983.

> This book is part of the WORLD MYTHOLOGY series.

Singh, Daljit, and Angela Smith. *The Sikh World.* Silver Burdett, 1983.

> This book describes the origin, beliefs, places of worship, holy book, ceremonies, festivals, and special signs of the Sikh faith.

Thompson, Brian. *The Story of Prince Rama.* Viking, 1985.

> This classic Asian epic of heroic Prince Rama's adventure is beautifully illustrated with reproductions of paintings from ancient manuscripts.

6.5   East Meets West: Rome

Asimov, Isaac. *The Roman Empire.* Houghton, 1967.

> This is an account of the 500-year period during which Rome established her empire—the events, the people, and the issues of the times. See also *The Roman Republic* by the same author.

Aurelius, Marcus. *Meditations.* Penguin, 1964.

> The musings and maxims of a Roman emperor who was trained in Stoicism are easily excerpted from this work.

The Bible. Various translations.

> Portions of the New Testament are examined in this unit.

Bruns, Roger. *Julius Caesar.* Chelsea House, 1987.

> This is a biography of the famous Roman soldier and statesman.

Caselli, Giovanni. *The Roman Empire and the Dark Ages.* Bedrick, 1985.

> The historical silence concerning early technological development is broken in this book by presenting a wide range of the most common and important objects from Roman times to the medieval era. See also *A Roman Soldier* (Bedrick, 1986) by the same author.

Corbishley, Mike. *The Roman World.* Warwick, 1986.

> This book takes a comprehensive look at the Roman world. It examines the republic, the empire, sports and leisure, public and community life, everyday life, crafts, and trade.

Crampton, William. *Eyewitness Books: Flags.* Knopf, 1989.

> Although the bulk of this book contains material related to later history, it faithfully and colorfully reproduces the Roman vexillum, the first true flag.

Dillon, Ellis. *Rome Under the Emperors.* Thomas Nelson, 1974.

> A view of life in Rome in A.D. 110, this historical novel tells the stories of four boys.

En Tiempo de los Romanos. Leon, Spain: Everest (Colección Saber Más).

> Illustrations, maps, and photographs of early Roman civilization are included in this Spanish-language book.

The Firebringer and Other Great Stories: Fifty-Five Legends That Live Forever. Retold by Louis Untermeyer. Evans, 1968.

> This is a collection of the great myths and legends from the Western traditions. It contains the story of Julius Caesar. See also *The World's Great Stories: 55 Legends That Live Forever* (Evans, 1987) by the same reteller. Both are usable in more than one unit in grades six and seven.

García de Dios, J. M. *Vida de Jesús—Historias de Jesús Contadas a los Niños.* Leon, Spain: Everest, 1982.

The life of Jesus of Nazareth is related in Spanish for young readers.

Glubok, Shirley. *The Art of Ancient Rome.* Harper, 1965.

Glubok describes Roman mosaics, murals, portraits, statuary, buildings, and monuments.

Goor, Ron, and Nancy Goor. *Pompeii: Exploring a Roman Ghost Town.* Crowell, 1986.

A concise overview of the social, political, cultural, and religious life in the ancient and ill-fated city of Pompeii is presented in this book.

Haugaard, Erik Christian. *The Rider and His Horse.* Houghton, 1968.

This is the story of David ben Joseph, a young man living in Jerusalem at the time of the Roman conquest.

Isenberg, J. *Julio César.* Barcelona: Timun Más (Hombres y Países), n.d.

This is a Spanish-language biography of the famous Roman emperor.

James, Simon. *Rome, 750 B.C.–500 A.D.* Watts, 1987.

In this book, a very brief text, enhanced by colorful illustrations, traces the history of Rome from an insignificant town in the eighth century B.C. to an empire.

Macaulay, David. *City: A Story of Roman Planning and Construction.* Houghton, 1983.

The text and black-and-white illustrations in this book show how the Romans planned and constructed their cities for the people who lived within them.

May, Robin. *Julius Caesar and the Romans.* Watts, 1984.

This book is an interesting blend of biography and history.

Odijk, Pamela. *The Romans.* Silver Burdett, 1989.

Time lines, good color photographs, and clear format make this book a valuable source for studying the cultural aspects of ancient Rome. This title is from THE ANCIENT WORLD, a series of books incorporating the Aztecs, Chinese, Israelites, Japanese, and others.

Purdy, Susan. *Ancient Rome.* Watts, 1982.

This book briefly describes the development of Roman civilization and gives directions for creating various artifacts.

Rutland, Jonathan. *See Inside a Roman Town.* Warwick, 1986.

Included in this book are views of a Roman town: the temple, shops, baths, theater, homes, places of business, and war technology. Readers will be transported over time to relive for themselves life in ancient Roman days. The SEE INSIDE series includes several worthwhile tales.

Speare, Elizabeth. *The Bronze Bow.* Houghton, 1961.

Set in Roman-occupied Palestine, this is the story of eighteen-year-old Daniel bar Jamin. Daniel wants vengeance against his Roman conquerors for the deaths of his father, uncle, and mother, as well as for his bondage to a vile blacksmith.

Story Bible. Various editions.

Retellings from the Gospels, the Acts of the Apostles, and the Book of Revelation are included in many collections.

Sutcliff, Rosemary. *The Eagle of the Ninth.* Oxford University Press, 1987.

In this story of Roman Britain in A.D.130, Marcus, a Roman Briton, sets out to search for his father, a member of the lost Legion of the Ninth. This book is the first of a trilogy.

Vanagas, Patricia. *Imperial Rome.* Gloucester, 1978.

Aspects of life in the Roman Empire from 27 B.C. until A.D. 138, focusing on the reign of Trajan, are described in this book.

Walworth, Nancy. *Augustus Caesar.* Chelsea House, 1989.

This is a new biography portraying the Roman emperor.

Windrow, Martin. *The Roman Legionary.* Watts, 1986.

Colored drawings enhance the concise text in this book and give readers a true picture of the life of the early Roman soldier.

Worm, Piet. *La Biblia Ilustrada.* Barcelona: Plaza y Janes, n.d.

    This illustrated Bible contains Spanish-language New Testament stories.

Yarbro, Chelsea Quinn. *Locadio's Apprentice.* Harper, 1984.

    Young Enecus Cano's dream seems to come true when he is accepted as an apprentice to physician Locadio Priscus. Set in the final days of ancient Pompeii, this book illustrates Roman social and family life and the surprisingly sophisticated state of Roman medical science.

Grade Seven: World History and Geography—Medieval and Early Modern Times

7.1 Connecting with Past Learnings: Uncovering the Remote Past

Anderson, Joan. *From Map to Museum: Uncovering Mysteries of the Past.* Morrow, 1988.

An archaeological expedition to St. Catherine's Island off the Georgia coast is described in this book. Artifacts found there are followed from discovery to display.

Arnold, Guy. *Book of Dates: A Chronology of World History.* Warwick, 1989.

Applicable to many units, this book gives thorough time lines that trace aspects of human development. Good visuals are included in this valuable resource.

Gallant, Roy. *Lost Cities.* Watts, 1985.

This book examines certain lost cities and describes how they were destroyed or abandoned and how they were rediscovered.

Irwin, Constance. *Strange Footprints on the Land: Vikings in America.* Harper, 1980.

The detective work that historians are doing to determine whether Vikings inhabited North America during the five centuries prior to Columbus is presented in this book.

Lyttle, Richard B. *Land Beyond the River: Europe in the Age of Migration.* Atheneum, 1987.

Vandals, Goths, Huns, Vikings, Muslims, Moguls, Anglos, and Saxons come to life along with Ghengis Khan, Alfred the Great, Muhammad, and Attila in this history of second- through ninth-century Europe. See also *The Games They Played: Sports in History* and *People of the Dawn: Early Man in the Americas.*

McLeish, Kenneth. *The Seven Wonders of the World.* Cambridge University Press, 1989.

This book gives each of the seven wonders of the world a chapter with historical background and a description of construction. The choice of the structures included is explained in the introduction.

Marston, Elsa. *Mysteries in American Archaeology.* Walker, 1986.

This book takes a look at the available facts and the clues to some of our strangest and still-unsolved archaeological puzzles.

Stuart, Gene. *Secrets from the Past.* National Geographic, 1979.

In this book, the reader learns how secrets of the ancient past are uncovered and what we know about our ancestors.

7.2 Connecting with Past Learnings: The Fall of Rome

Fagg, Christopher. *Ancient Rome.* Warwick, 1978.

The civilization of the Romans, whose empire dominated the Western world for 500 years, is discussed in this book.

Hadas, Moses. *Imperial Rome.* Time-Life Books, 1965.

Rome grew from a collection of prehistoric villages to a worldwide empire. This book describes how a strong sense of order and the infusion of the cultural and technical achievements of assimilated peoples gave shape to the state and empire.

Hughes, Jill. *Imperial Rome.* Watts, 1985.

This book provides an overview of imperial Rome with an emphasis on politics but with little about daily life and customs.

Seredy, Kate. *The White Stag.* Penguin, 1935.

This collection of Hungarian folktales contains the story of the early days of the Hungarian people when the Huns and Magyars roamed Europe.

Sutcliff, Rosemary. *The Lantern Bearers.* Oxford, 1979.

In this historical adventure invading bands of Saxons, Jutes, Scots, and Picts harry the people of

Britain in the fifth century. The action of this novel takes place just after the departure of the Roman legions and shows how peoples from enemy groups gradually merged. See also *Frontier Wolf* and *Song for a Dark Queen* by the same author.

7.3 The Growth of Islam

Aggarwal, Manju. *I Am a Muslim.* Watts, 1985.

A brief, well-illustrated introduction to Muslims' beliefs and culture is provided in this book through the eyes of an eleven-year-old boy.

Agullo, Carmen. *Las Mil y Una Noches.* Madrid: Edaf, 1984.

This is a Spanish translation of the famous *Arabian Nights* tales.

Ali Baba and the Forty Thieves. Illustrated by Margaret Early. Abrams, 1989.

Visually splendid, this picture book has a narrative that is within the grasp of most seventh graders.

The Arabian Nights Entertainments. Retold by Andrew Lang. Dover reprint, 1969.

Included in the book are the best-known tales that the resourceful and loquacious Scheherazade told her brutal sultan. Lang is a nineteenth-century folklorist, and students should hear and read his language.

Beshore, George. *Science in Early Islamic Culture.* Watts, 1988.

One of the noteworthy SCIENCE IN . . . series, this book contributes to the study of cultural literacy in this unit.

"The City of Ultimate Beauty and Happiness," in *Legends of Journeys.* Retold by Olga Norris. Cambridge University Press, 1988.

This Persian folktale tells of Aziz, who becomes obsessed with a tale of a city of happiness. The book is an attractive collection that contains stories applicable to other units.

Duckworth, John. *Muhammad and the Arab Empire.* Greenhaven, 1980.

This is the story of the great religious leader whose words swept through the Arab world and across the East as far as Java, bringing into being the mighty force known as Islam.

Finkelstein, Norman. *The Other 1492: Jewish Settlement in the New World.* Scribner, 1989.

The story of Jewish expulsion from Spain is a little-know incident in world history. The author's detailed account broadens students' understanding of this historical period. The book is included here because it touches on the Al-Andalus, a Moslem kingdom.

Gibb, H. A. R. *Mohammedanism: An Historical Survey.* Oxford, 1953.

This teacher's resource is an overview of Islamic religion and its impact on the Mediterranean basin. It covers Mohammedan orthodoxy and various sects.

Khayyam, Omar. *The Rubaiyat.* Airmont (or other paperback), 1969.

The best-known English version of this collection of quatrains by the twelfth-century Persian poet is the translation by Edward FitzGerald. The edition published by Penguin and translated in 1984 by Peter Avery and John Heath-Stubbs probably retains more of the skepticism of the original.

The Koran. Various publishers and dates.

Several translations of this basic Islamic holy book are available. Perhaps the most inexpensive edition is N. J. Dawood's translation for Penguin paperbacks. Others, such as those translated by Mir Ahmad Ali and H. M. Shakir, are available from Tahrike Tarsile Quran. Consult *Books in Print* or Islamic scholars for additional choices.

Mayer, Marianna. *Aladdin and the Enchanted Lamp.* Macmillan, 1985.

This is a well-told, illustrated version of the tale from the *Arabian Nights*.

Moktefi, Mokhtar. *Rise of Islam.* Silver Burdett, 1987.

The spread of Islam is shown in this book from its beginnings in the seventh century and throughout its colorful history. This book is currently out of print.

Tames, Richard. *The Muslim World.* Silver Burdett, 1983.

Included in this book are the history, principles, and customs of Islam, including the life of Muhammad; a discussion of the Koran and the five pillars of Islam; and a discussion of the efforts of Islamic countries to remain traditional in a modern world.

Wolkstein, Diane. *The Red Lion: A Persian Story.* Crowell, 1977.

In this tale of ancient Persia, a prince runs away on the eve of his coronation because he fears lions. The illustrations in this book are heavily influenced by Islamic manuscript paintings.

7.4   African States in the Middle Ages and Early Modern Times

Brooks, Lester. *Great Civilizations of Ancient Africa.* Four Winds, 1971.

A survey of the black civilizations that flourished throughout the continent of Africa, this book contains maps, photographs, a chronology, a bibliography, and an index that make it an invaluable source.

Carpenter, Allan. *Benin.* Children's Press, 1978.

The history, geography, people, culture, and government of Benin, a small agricultural country on the west coast of Africa, are introduced in this book. See also *Gambia, Liberia, Mauritania,* and *Togo* from the same series.

Chu, Daniel. *A Glorious Age in Africa: The Story of Three Great African Empires.* Doubleday, 1965.

The three empires of the title are Ghana, Mali, and Songhay, which flourished 1,000 years ago in central Africa.

Davidson, Basil. *African Kingdoms.* Time-Life Books, 1966.

This is a description of great African cultures profusely illustrated by an Africanist. Included are an index, a chronology, and a bibliography.

Knappert, Jan. *Kings, Gods, and Spirits from African Mythology.* Schocken, 1986.

Part of the WORLD MYTHOLOGY series, this carefully researched book offers historical background and appealing illustrations as it presents African myths and folktales. A chapter devoted to African fables is included. Unlike some collections, the language and format are not beneath the maturity level of middle school students.

McEvedy, Colin. *Atlas of African History.* Penguin, 1980.

This is a handy historical atlas that supplements studies in this and earlier units in world history.

Reese, Lyn. *Spindle Stories.* Women in the World, 1990.

Since the roles and voices of Songhay and Hausa women are not often included in world history classes, this resource is a helpful one to teachers. Also included are stories of Pompeii and of Renaissance Florence that make the book usable in other units. In addition to the stories, activities and questions are suggested.

Warren, Fred. *Music of Africa.* Prentice Hall, 1970.

Amply illustrated with photographs and line drawings, the text of this book introduces the music of Africa in an authoritative and comprehensive manner.

7.5   Civilizations of the Americas

Beck, Barbara. *The Aztecs.* Watts, 1983.

This book describes some of the achievements of the Aztec civilization and includes instructions for reproducing various Aztec artifacts.

Blassingame, Wyatt. *The Incas and the Spanish Conquest.* Messner, 1980.

The Inca civilization in Peru and its destruction by the Spanish are described in this book.

Fisher, Leonard. *Pyramid of the Sun—Pyramid of the Moon.* Macmillan, 1988.

The Toltec and Aztec cultures are carefully described and enhanced by memorable illustrations in this book.

"Four Creations to Make Man," in *In the Beginning: Creation Stories from Around the World.* Retold by Virginia Hamilton. Harcourt, 1988.

This creation myth from Mayan culture was almost lost; fortunately, it was transcribed.

Gifford, Douglas. *Warriors, Gods and Spirits from Central and South American Mythology.* Schocken, 1983.

> John Sibbick's illustrations for this folktale collection appeal to middle school students. Stories represent Aztec, Toltec, Mayan, Incan, and other cultures. The author includes helpful historical background.

Goldsmit, Gersón, and Shulamit Goldsmit. *La Civilización Maya.* Mexico City: Trillas, n.d.

> This Mayan history is best suited for slightly advanced Spanish readers.

Harris, Nathaniel. *Montezuma and the Aztecs.* Watts, 1986.

> This book explores the Aztec civilization through Montezuma's life.

Hughes, Jill. *Aztecs.* Watts, 1987.

> The rise and fall of the Aztec empire is traced and the empire's culture and beliefs are explored in this book.

Lattimore, Deborah Nourse. *The Flame of Peace.* Harper, 1987.

> In retelling this authentic Aztec tale, Lattimore reproduces icons and designs germane to this ancient culture. The story is based on the "Alliance of Cities" during the time of Itzcoatl. See also Lattimore's *Why There Is No Arguing in Heaven,* a book that is suitable for other topics in this unit.

Los Aztecas: Entre el Dios de la Lluvia y el de la Guerra. Madrid: Anaya (Biblioteca Iberoamericana), 1988.

> Spanish-language companion volumes, *Los Incas* and *Los Mayas,* are available from the same publisher.

McKissack, Pat. *Aztec Indians.* Children's Press, 1985.

> The Aztec Indians and their history, religion, language, customs, and final days are discussed in this book. See also *The Inca* by the same author.

Marrin, Albert. *Aztecs and Spaniards: Cortes and the Conquest of Mexico.* Atheneum, 1986.

> The culture of the Aztec Indians is brought to life in this book. The fall of the Aztecs' vast empire began with the arrival of Hernando Cortés in 1519. See also *Inca and Spaniard: Pizarro and the Conquest of Peru* (1989) by this author.

Meyer, Carolyn, and Charles Gallenkamp. *The Mystery of the Ancient Maya.* Atheneum, 1985.

> Written almost as a mystery story, this absorbing and fascinating book tells about discoveries of ancient Mayan cities in the jungles of Central America.

Millard, Anne. *The Incas.* Watts, 1980.

> This book discusses the Incas and their history, religion, language, and customs.

Morrison, Marion. *Atahualpa and the Incas.* Bookwright, 1986.

> A brief, well-written overview of the Incan empire at the time of the Spanish conquest is provided in this book.

O'Dell, Scott. *The Amethyst Ring.* Houghton, 1983.

> Julian Escobar, a Spaniard who is known by the name Kukulcan, witnesses the swift and tragic fall of the Incan empire. See also *The Feathered Serpent* by the same author. This novel may be used in unit 7.10.

Odijk, Pamela. *The Incas.* Silver Burdett, 1989.

> This is a colorful, clear presentation that serves as an introduction or as a resource for students' research. See also Odijk's *The Mayas* and *The Aztecs.*

Piggott, Juliet. *Mexican Folk Tales.* Crane Russak, 1973.

> The folklore of Mexico falls into two periods—pre- and postconquest. The first inhabitants produced myths and legends that explained the mysteries of the world's creation and the beauties of their natural world. The Spaniards brought a more sophisticated folklore that was imbued with European and Christian traditions. The two blended and formed a delightful heritage of tales.

Unstead, Robert. *See Inside an Aztec Town.* Warwick, 1980.

> This is a visually appealing book about the Aztec civilization.

Witlock, Ralph. *Everyday Life of the Maya.* Hippocrene Books, 1987.

> In this story of the Mayas at the height of their glory, Mayan clothes, food, colorful ceremonies, and human sacrifices are discussed. An excellent descrip-

tion of Mayan beliefs, literature, and social hierarchy is included.

7.6 China

Carpenter, Frances. *Tales of a Chinese Grandmother.* Charles E. Tuttle, 1972.

This is a collection of popular Chinese folktales.

Carter, Alden R. *Modern China.* Watts, 1986.

Black-and-white photographs and paintings enhance an excellent text that examines the history, customs, and social life of modern China.

Ceserani, Gian P. *Marco Polo.* Putnam, 1982.

This book follows the adventures of the thirteenth-century Venetian merchant who wrote a famous account of his travels in Asia and his life in the court of Kublai Khan.

Filstrup, Chris, and Janie Filstrup. *China, from Emperors to Communes.* Dillon, 1983.

Facts about Chinese history, art, traditions, social life, and recreation are presented in this book.

Hoff, Rhoda. *China: Adventures in Eyewitness History.* Walck, 1965.

This book records firsthand accounts of historical events by ambassadors, missionaries, students, princes, merchants, and doctors. These accounts range from 651 B.C. to 1936.

Leaf, Margaret. *Eyes of the Dragon.* Lothrop, 1987.

A Chinese folktale is beautifully illustrated in this book.

McLenighan, Valjean. *China: A History to Nineteen Forty-Nine.* Children's Press, 1983.

The history until 1949 of the country with the oldest continuing history of any nation is presented in this book.

Marri, Noemi Vicini. *Marco Polo.* Silver Burdett, 1985.

This is another account of the adventures of the thirteenth-century Venetian merchant who traveled in Asia and lived at the court of Kublai Khan. See

also *Marco Polo* by Gian P. Ceserani (Putnam, 1982).

Polo, Marco. *The Travels of Marco Polo.* Various editions.

In addition to hardback form, several paperback editions of this travel classic are available (e.g., Airmont, Penguin, Signet NAL, and Silver Burdett).

Roberson, John R. *China from Manchu to Mao (1699–1976).* Atheneum, 1980.

This history of China begins in 1699 during the reign of Emperor Kang XI at a time when the influence of foreigners in China began to grow.

Saunders, Tao T. *Dragons, Gods and Spirits from Chinese Mythology.* Schocken, 1983.

This book is part of the World Mythology series.

Spencer, Cornelia. *Made in China.* Knopf, 1954.

This survey of Chinese arts and products contains chapters on calligraphy, T'ang painting, architecture, and more.

Young, Ed. *Lon Po Po.* Putnam, 1989.

This Chinese tale, akin to "Little Red Riding Hood," is impressively illustrated.

7.7 Japan

Balent, Matthew. *The Palladium Book of Weapons and Castles of the Orient.* Palladium Books, 1984.

This work is helpful when comparing medieval Japan and Europe.

Byam, Michele. *Arms and Armor.* Knopf, 1988.

Sharp, detailed photographs provide colorful primary sources for this unit as well as others in the world history course for the sixth and seventh grades. The unusual presentation of Samurai armory in this book justifies its inclusion here.

Davidson, Judith. *Japan, Where East Meets West.* Dillon, 1983.

An introduction to the history and culture of Japan is provided in this book.

Greene, Carol. *Japan.* Children's Press, 1983.

Some of Japan's geography, history, scenic treasures, culture, industry, and people are described in this book.

Haugaard, Erik. *The Samurai's Tale.* Houghton, 1984.

This the story of a Japanese orphan boy, Tara, who becomes a samurai in sixteenth-century Japan.

Hutt, Julia. *Understanding Far Eastern Art.* Dutton, 1987.

Many art examples from this teacher's resource can be shown in class.

James, Grace. *Japanese Fairy Tales.* Smith reprint, 1923.

This is an enduring collection of captivating tales.

McAlpine, Helen. *Japanese Tales and Legends.* Oxford, 1989.

This is a new paperback reprint of a standard collection.

Murasaki, Lady. *The Tale of Genji.* Random, 1985.

This *MODERN LIBRARY* edition is one of the classics in world literature. It has been called "the world's first novel." It is lengthy and requires excerpting.

Ozaki, Yei Theodora. *The Japanese Fairy Book.* C. E. Tuttle, 1970.

This paperbound edition is a valuable resource for classroom use. A costly library binding edition is available from Gordon Press.

Paterson, Katherine. *The Sign of the Chrysanthemum.* Crowell, 1973.

The uniqueness of feudal Japan is captured in this book. Muna is a thirteen-year-old boy on a desperate search for the father he has never seen. See also *The Master Puppeteer* and *Of Nightingales That Weep* by the same author.

Piggott, Juliet. *Japanese Mythology* (Revised edition). Bedrick, 1983.

Japan is described in this book as a country rich in myths, legends, and folktales inspired by history, ghost stories, and religion. It is a useful teacher's resource.

Shimer, Dorothy Blair. *Rice Bowl Women.* New American Library, 1982.

The role of women in Asian cultures is discussed in this teacher's resource.

7.8 Medieval Societies: Europe and Japan

Andronik, Catherine M. *Quest for a King: Searching for the Real King Arthur.* Atheneum, 1989.

This engaging search for historical verification of the legendary Arthur is enhanced by geographical, literary, and anthropological material. The book includes good visuals.

Beowulf. Translated by Michael Alexander. Penguin, 1973.

This is only one of several translations available. Excerpts are recommended in the framework for contrast with Japanese haiku.

Brett, Bernard. *The Fighting Ship.* Oxford, 1988.

A full account of the organization and function of this military unit is given in this book.

Brooks, Polly Schoyer, and Nancy Zinsser Walworth. *The World of Walls: The Middle Ages in Western Europe.* Lippincott, 1966.

A series of biographical sketches in this book provides a vivid picture of the era of barbarian invasions, feudalism, knights, and the Crusades. See also Brooks's *Queen Eleanor: Independent Spirit of the Medieval World.*

Carrick, Donald. *Harald and the Giant Knight.* Clarion, 1982.

This picture book and its companion, *Harald and the Great Stag,* present the European feudal system in an unromantic light. The hard lives of the serfs were subject to the whims of their barons.

Caselli, Giovanni. *A Medieval Monk.* Bedrick, 1986.

This easily read book describes the life of a monk in a medieval monastery.

Caselli, Giovanni. *El Imperio Romano y la Europa Medioeval.* Madrid: Generales Anaya (Colección La Vida en el Pasado), n.d.

This is a Spanish-language history of ancient Rome and the Middle Ages.

Chaucer, Geoffrey. *Canterbury Tales.* Translated by Barbara Cohen. Lothrop, 1988.

These are the tales of pilgrims who traveled to Canterbury in the Middle Ages to visit the shrine of St. Thomas à Becket.

Clarke, Richard. *Castles.* Bookwright, 1986.

Various kinds of castles are described in this book that explains how and why they were built, what life in them was like, and how they were defended.

Davis, Mary. *Women Who Changed History: Five Famous Queens of Europe.* Lerner, 1975.

This book contains biographical portraits of Eleanor of Aquitaine, Isabella of Spain, Elizabeth of England, Marie Antoinette of France, and Catherine the Great of Russia.

Day, James. *The Black Death.* Bookwright, 1989.

The story of this great disaster is presented with simple narrative and illustrations in this book. The book provides much pertinent information in a brief account. It depicts people and events and quotes primary sources.

De Angeli, Marguerite. *The Door in the Wall: Story of Medieval London.* Doubleday, 1949.

Set in 1325, this is the tale of ten-year-old Robin, who, ill and unable to walk, acquires strength and courage.

Denny, Norman, and Josephine Filmer-Sankey. *The Bayeux Tapestry: The Norman Conquest of 1066.* Parkwest, 1988.

A most extraordinary account of history is contained on a magnificent tapestry, 230 feet (70.1 metres) long. A remarkable achievement of art and handicraft from the middle ages is described in this book.

Fisher, Leonard Everett. *The Tower of London.* Macmillan, 1987.

This picture book is prepared in an appealing manner that motivates youngsters to study the historical period.

Funcken, Liliane. *The Age of Chivalry.* Prentice Hall, 1983.

The magnificent illustrations, maps, and superb text in this book bring to life the color, the poetry, and the creativity of a period rich in human drama.

Gray, Elizabeth. *Adam of the Road.* Viking, 1942.

This story of thirteenth-century England is a light-hearted tale of an eleven-year-old boy who wanders the minstrels' road, meeting noblemen, farmers, and pilgrims.

Green, Roger Lancelyn. *King Arthur and His Knights of the Round Table.* Penguin Puffin, 1974.

Another worthwhile retelling of the classic legend is found in this book. See also *Adventures of Robin Hood.*

Hodges, Margaret. *Saint George and the Dragon.* Little, Brown, 1984.

This picture book presents the famous legend of a young knight's fight with a horrible dragon.

Hollister, C. Warren, and others. *Medieval Europe: A Short Sourcebook.* McGraw-Hill, 1982.

Students as well as teachers can use this book of primary sources.

Holme, Bryan. *Medieval Pageant.* Thames and Hudson, 1987.

This is a visually splendid volume depicting art and pageantry from the Middle Ages. All the art is authentic and stunningly reproduced.

Kelly, Eric P. *The Trumpeter of Krakow.* Macmillan, 1966.

This is a mystery adventure involving Polish people and set in the fifteenth century during the Renaissance.

Kipling, Rudyard. *Puck of Pook's Hill.* Penguin, 1987.

The elfin Puck relates fictional stories rooted in the history of medieval and earlier times. G. M. Trevelyan praised Kipling's "marvelous historical sense."

Konigsburg, E. L. *A Proud Taste for Scarlet and Miniver.* Atheneum, 1973.

This is the story of Eleanor of Aquitaine as she reflects on her life.

Lanier, Sidney. *The Boy's King Arthur.* Scribner, 1989.

Handsome binding and illustrations enhance this

durable retelling of Thomas Mallory's medieval legend.

Lasker, Joe. *A Tournament of Knights.* Crowell, 1986.

A young knight is challenged to his first tournament by Sir Rolf, an experienced jouster. The activities and preparations leading to the tournament are described, including the customs and terminology of the times.

Lebrun, Francoise. *The Days of Charlemagne.* Translated by Christopher Sharp, illustrated by Ginette Hoffmann. Silver Burdett, 1986.

In simple and brief text, the medieval world is explored through the fictional life of a young boy, Gerald, who is pursuing his studies in a monastery.

Lewis, Naomi. *Proud Knight, Fair Lady: The Twelve Lais of Marie de France.* Viking, 1989.

In the twelfth century, poet Marie de France collected fairy tales from traveling minstrels. Lewis is a master storyteller and offers sensitive translations and background information.

Macaulay, David. *Castle.* Houghton, 1982.

A distinguished and thorough work that describes the floor plans, laborers, tools, construction, defense, and decline of a medieval castle. See also Macaulay's *Cathedral: The Story of Its Construction.*

McEvedy, Colin. *The Penguin Atlas of Medieval History.* Penguin, 1986.

Seventh-grade students and their teachers will find this historical atlas a trove of information that is suitable for this unit.

McKinley, Robin. *The Outlaws of Sherwood.* Greenwillow, 1988.

In this story of Robin Hood and his merry men and women, Maid Marian helps a troubled Robin overcome self-doubts and adjust to life in the forest as a Saxon renegade who has abandoned polite, upper-crust Norman English society.

Meltzer, Milton. *Columbus and the World Around Him.* Watts, 1990.

Meltzer's biography of the great explorer is better used as background material for teachers. Advanced

students might enjoy some of the illustrations. In this book, Meltzer depicts the cultural milieu in which Columbus lived.

Miquel, Pierre. *The Days of Knights and Castles.* Silver Burdett, 1985.

This book contains standard historical and cultural data with colorful illustrations. See Philippe Brochard's *Castles of the Middle Ages,* also from Silver Burdett's *Picture Histories* series.

Morgan, Gwyneth. *Life in a Medieval Village.* Lerner, 1982.

The various aspects of life in a thirteenth-century English village are described in this book. Included are housing; food; dress; occupations; laws; the roles of the church; and the activities of the serfs, farmers, and the lord and lady of the manor.

Oakes, Catherine. *Exploring the Past: The Middle Ages.* Harcourt, 1989.

Everyday life in medieval times and the richness and complexity of the period come through in this book. Other titles in the *Exploring the Past* series are usable in several units and are attractive resources.

Picard, Barbara. *One Is One.* Holt, 1966.

Set in medieval England, this story traces the life of Stephen de Beaurille from the time he is nine years of age in 1318 until 1335 when he rejects his knighthood to return to the monastery to paint for God. See also *Ransom for a Knight.*

Pope, Elizabeth. *The Perilous Gard.* Houghton, 1974.

In 1558, Queen Mary relocates Kate Sutton from Hatfield House, where she has been serving Princess Elizabeth, to Sir Geoffrey's Elvenwood Hall, known as the "perilous gard."

Pyle, Howard. *The Merry Adventures of Robin Hood.* Scribner, 1946.

This is a classic account of the unforgettable plunderer. Scribner's also publishes a version by Paul Creswick, which is illustrated by N. C. Wyeth. See also Pyle's *Story of King Arthur and His Knights* (Scribner), *Otto of the Silver Hand* (Dover), *Men of Iron* (Airmont), and *King Arthur* (Scribner). These books are perhaps better suited for advanced readers.

Ross, Stewart. *A Crusading Knight.* Rourke, 1987.

> The background of the Crusades and the day-to-day life of knights who pledged to fight in them are described in this book. Included are the final outcomes of their campaigns.

Sancha, Sheila. *The Luttrell Village: Country Life in the Middle Ages.* Crowell, 1983.

> This book traces the social life and customs of fourteenth-century England in a Lincolnshire village from plowing through harvesting. Magnificent full-page illustrations accompany the text.

Serraillier, Ian. *Beowulf, the Warrior.* Walck, 1961.

> This is a powerful retelling in rhyme of the heroic saga of a man gaining victory over a formidable foe.

Sutcliff, Rosemary. *The Light Beyond the Forest: The Quest for the Holy Grail.* Dutton, 1980.

> The adventures of King Arthur's knights are retold in this book. Sir Lancelot, Sir Galahad, Sir Bors, and Sir Percival search for the Holy Grail. See also *Road to Camlann* and *The Sword and the Circle*, both by Sutcliff.

Trease, Geoffrey. *The Red Towers of Granada.* Vanguard, 1967.

> Set in England and Spain around 1290 during the reign of Edward I, this is the story of Robin, who has been declared a leper by the village's priest and sails to Spain to find a cure. See also *Escape to King Alfred* and *The Baron's Hostage* by the same author.

Van Woerkom, Dorothy. *Pearl in the Egg: A Tale of the Thirteenth Century.* Crowell, 1980.

> This book is based on the life of Pearl, who becomes a minstrel in the court of Edward I of England. Together with her brother, she runs away from serfdom to join a troop of traveling entertainers. This book is out of print, but libraries may have copies.

Von Canon, Claudia. *The Inheritance.* Houghton, 1983.

> This story is set in Spain during the Spanish Inquisition.

Windrow, Martin, and Richard Hook. *The Foot Soldier.* Oxford, 1988.

> This book and its companion, *The Horse Soldier*, offer clear and entertaining discussions of two kinds of fighting men throughout history.

Wright, Sylvia. *The Age of Chivalry in English Society, 1200–1400.* Warwick, 1988.

> This well-illustrated book provides an attractive format for historical information.

7.9   Europe During the Renaissance, the Reformation, and the Scientific Revolution

Anderson, David. *The Spanish Armada.* Hampstead Press, 1988.

> This appealing book provides facts and details of this fated fleet.

Asimov, Isaac. *Great Ideas of Science.* Houghton, 1969.

> The historic development of important scientific ideas is the subject of this book. The contribution of each theory or discovery to the development of scientific thought and method is analyzed.

Beatty, John, and Patricia Beatty. *Master Rosalind.* Morrow, 1974.

> Elizabethan England is the setting for this story of twelve-year-old Rosalind, who, on a journey for her grandfather, is kidnapped and forced to become a thief in London. Her adventures take her into the lives of Shakespeare's actors and involve her in court intrigue.

Berenson, Bernard. *Italian Painters of the Renaissance.* Cornell University Press, 1980.

> This teacher's resource contains art history pertinent to this unit of study.

Bowen, Catherine Drinker. *Francis Bacon: The Temper of a Man.* Little, Brown, 1963.

> An engrossing portrait by a popular, meticulous biographer, this book provides useful background material for teachers.

Brown, John R. *Shakespeare and His Theatre.* Lothrop, 1982.

This work describes what we now believe William Shakespeare's Globe Theater was like. Also check the library for Anne Terry White's *Will Shakespeare and the Globe Theater* (Random, Landmark, 1955).

Bunyan, John. *Pilgrim's Progress.* Dodd, Mead, 1979.

This edition is from the GREAT ILLUSTRATED CLASSICS series. Bunyan's work is possibly the most influential allegory in Western literature. The reading level is challenging for seventh graders; James Reeves's retelling (CHILDREN'S CLASSICS FROM WORLD LITERATURE series, Bedrick, 1987) may be more appropriate.

Caselli, Giovanni. *The Renaissance and the New World.* Bedrick, 1986.

In discussing Renaissance events and attitudes, this book depicts a range of people whose ways of life reveal the society that developed in Europe and America from the fifteenth century into the eighteenth century. Long-distance trade and international commerce, new technologies, and discoveries are discussed. See also Caselli's *A German Printer.*

Cobb, Vicki. *Truth on Trial: The Story of Galileo Galilei.* Coward, 1979.

This is a biography of the great mathematician and physicist who was tried by the Inquisition for challenging the accepted theories of his day.

Cottler, Joseph, and Jaffee Cottler. *34 Biografías de Científicos y Exploradores, Héroes de la Civilización.* Mexico: Libro-Mex Editores, 1981.

Biographical portraits of prominent figures in history, including explorers, are presented in this Spanish-language book.

de la Helguera, A. *Gutenberg.* Leon, Spain: Araluce (Los Grandes Hombres), n.d.

This is a Spanish-language biography of the great printer who changed the course of history.

Despois, Pauline J. *La Vida de un Artista Florentino en la Epoca del Renacimiento.* Madrid: Altea, 1981.

The life of a Florentine artist of the Renaissance is discussed here in Spanish.

Eliot, George. *Romola.* Penguin, 1980.

Lengthy and better suited for advanced readers, this book tells of a strong heroine's life. It is set in Florence at the time of Savonarola and the Medicis' decline.

Foxe, John. *Foxe's Book of Martyrs.* Various editions.

Minister John Foxe (1516–1587), sometimes spelled "Fox," was a student of Christian martyrs throughout history. This work has been widely read for its depiction of Protestant Reformation martyrdom. Excerpts from this teacher's resource could be useful.

Galileo. Madrid: Edaf (Colección Por Qué Se Hicieron Famosos), 1983.

This Spanish-language biography is suitable for middle school and early high school readers. This is part of a series that also contains books about Leonardo da Vinci and Marco Polo.

Harris, Nathaniel. *Leonardo and the Renaissance.* Watts, 1987.

The brief text of this book accompanies colorful illustrations of a period that produced great thinkers and painters and marked the beginning of the modern world.

Herrera, Juan Ignacio. *Miguel de Cervantes.* Spain: Susaeta, 1981.

This is a Spanish-language biography of the great Spanish novelist whose *Don Quixote* is a world masterpiece.

Hibbard, Howard. *Michelangelo.* Harper, 1975.

In this biography, Michelangelo becomes a living personality, and his life story is revealed through his own works of art, which are reproduced in 31 photographs. See also *Rembrandt, A Biography* and *Titian, A Biography.*

Hibbert, Christopher. *The House of Medici: Its Rise and Fall.* Morrow, 1980.

Useful as background material for teachers, this paperbound book is a lengthy, informative account of Florentine history and culture.

Hilgartner, Beth. *A Murder for Her Majesty.* Houghton, 1986.

Horrified at having witnessed her father's murder and fearing that the killers are agents of Queen Elizabeth I, eleven-year-old Alice Tuckfield hides in

Yorkshire Cathedral by disguising herself as one of the choirboys.

Ipsen, D. C. *Isaac Newton, Reluctant Genius.* Enslow, 1985.

Gravity, light and color, and the system of calculus are today within human understanding because of the work of this great scientist.

Kingsley, Charles. *Westward Ho!* Buccaneer Books or Airmont, various dates.

This nineteenth-century English classic of historical fiction is set in the milieu of Elizabeth I and William Shakespeare. It is recommended for advanced readers.

Koestler, Arthur. *The Watershed: A Biography of Johannes Kepler.* University Press of America, 1985.

This reprint of Anchor's 1960 publication is useful as background material for teachers.

McRae, Lee. *Handbook of the Renaissance.* Elementary-Secondary Education Committee, 1989.

This paperbound book is a concise, well-researched manual and a useful teacher's resource. Aspects of life, culture, women's roles, and exploration during the Renaissance are described. Helpful lists of readings and recordings are provided.

Nesbit, E. *The Children's Shakespeare.* Random, 1968.

This is a reprint of a 1930s title that deserves republication. Nesbit's retellings are short and have a style that some readers will find inviting.

O'Dell, Scott. *The Road to Damietta.* Houghton, 1985.

Through the eyes of a young woman, we witness the transformation of a pleasure-seeking young man into the joyous man who sought to bring the world into loving harmony—St. Francis of Assisi.

O'Neill, Judith. *Martin Luther.* Lerner, 1979.

This is one of the few biographies for young readers that deals with this Reformation crusader.

Papp, Joseph, and Elizabeth Kirkland. *Shakespeare Alive!* Bantam, 1988.

A good presentation of cultural and everyday life in the England of Elizabeth I is contained in this book.

Raboff, Ernest. *Albrecht Durer.* Harper, 1988.

This book is one of an outstanding series that integrates history, culture, and art. See also Raboff's books on Michelangelo, Rembrandt, da Vinci, and Raphael.

Scholderer, Victor. *Johann Gutenberg, the Inventor of Printing* (Revised edition). Longwood Publishing Group, 1970.

This teacher's resource offers a brief, illustrated discussion of an inventor who changed the world.

Shakespeare for Young People. Edited by Diane Davidson. Swan Books.

This series of plays is listed here for purposes of correlation with English–language arts. The editor has remained faithful to William Shakespeare's language but has made the complexities of his dramas understandable for students. All plays offered are within a realistic length of time for reading or performing. Information on particular titles can be obtained from the publisher.

Shakespeare's Stories: Histories. Retold by Beverley Birch. Bedrick, 1988.

Birch's retellings preserve the spirit of William Shakespeare's original dramas. Also available by the same author and publisher are *Shakespeare's Stories: Comedies* and *Shakespeare's Stories: Tragedies.*

Van Loon, Hendrik. *The Life and Times of Rembrandt.* Liveright, 1943.

Although not written for juvenile readers, this book contains useful information.

Ventura, Piero. *Venice: Birth of a City.* Putnam, 1988.

The development of this Adriatic city is highlighted in this book. Included are the city's pageantry, festivals, and architecture.

Ventura, Piero, and Gian Carlo Ceserani. *El Viaje de Marco Polo.* Madrid: Magisterio Español, 1979.

Polo's famous journey to Eastern lands is detailed in this Spanish-language volume.

Vining, Elizabeth. *I Will Adventure.* Viking, 1962.

Andrew Talbot, age twelve years, leaves his family in 1596 to be a page for his cousin, Sir John, in London. On the way from Canterbury to London, he stops at an inn where players are presenting *Romeo and Juliet*. This experience changes his life—he is caught up in the world of William Shakespeare. This book deserves republication.

7.10 Early Modern Europe: The Age of Exploration to the Enlightenment

Aliki. *The King's Day: Louis XIV of France*. Crowell, 1989.

Although intended for a younger audience, this sophisticated picture book is worth examining. Well researched, it depicts the outgrowth of the *divine right* concept and uses French terms in discussing daily life at Versailles. Art prints and the music of Francois Couperin can be used to extend the study.

Buehr, Walter. *The Portuguese Explorers*. Putnam, 1966.

Portugal's domination of the seas in the fifteenth century is covered in this book. The thrill of discovery is depicted through the voyages of Bartholomeu Dias, Vasco da Gama, and Prince Henry the Navigator.

Cairns, Trevor. *Birth of Modern Europe*. Lerner, 1975.

The political, cultural, and religious movements that occurred in Europe between 1500 and 1715 are highlighted in this book.

Calvert, Patricia. *Hadder MacColl*. Scribner, 1985.

This novel is set in the Scottish highlands in 1745 and 1746. It centers on the Jacobite Rebellion and the Battle of Culloden and is told by the fourteen-year-old daughter of a highland chieftain.

Castillo, Bernal del. *Cortez and the Conquest of Mexico by the Spaniards in 1521*. Abridged by B. G. Herzog. Linnet Books, 1988.

This is the eyewitness account of Bernal Díaz del Castillo under the leadership of Hernando Cortés in Mexico.

Connaty, Mary. *The Armada*. Warwick, 1988.

The events that led to the dispatch of the Spanish Armada and the conflict between England and Spain are discussed in this book.

La Conquista de México Según las Ilustraciones del Códice Florentino. Edited by Marta Dujovne. Mexico City: Nueva Imagen, 1978.

This history of the conquest of Mexico is told from the point of view of the conquered Nahuatl Indians. Accounts are based on the hieroglyphic history of the Nahuatl. Brief Spanish explanations of each picture tell the story in words.

Daugherty, James. *The Magna Charta*. Random, LANDMARK SERIES, 1956.

This book briefly describes life in twelfth-century England and the rule of Richard, events leading to the Magna Charta, and milestones in constitutional law since 1215. It is usable also at Unit 8.1, and it is deserving of republication.

Defoe, Daniel. *Robinson Crusoe*. Illustrated by N. C. Wyeth. Scribner, 1983.

This is not only a grand story but also one of the best depictions of navigation, world places, spirituality, and culture of the 1600s.

Garfield, Leon. *The Night of the Comet*. Delacourt, 1979.

These haunting tales of eighteenth-century London provide excellent outside reading for students, with images of political, social, and cultural conditions of the time. See also *Smith; Footsteps: A Novel;* and *The December Rose* by the same author.

Grant, Neil. *Everyday Life in the Eighteenth Century*. Silver Burdett, 1983.

Everyday life in eighteenth-century Europe and the changes brought about by political, industrial, and agricultural revolutions are discussed in this book.

Haugaard, Erik Christian. *Cromwell's Boy*. Houghton, 1978.

Oliver Cutler, age thirteen, is a good horseman. Clever, reliable, and a spy for General Oliver Cromwell, he infiltrates the homes and hangouts of King Charles's advocates.

Howard, C. *Pizarro y la Conquista del Perú*. Barcelona: Timun Más (Hombres y Países), n.d.

This book is a good Spanish-language complement to Albert Marrin's English-language book on the same topic.

Ish-Kishor, Sulamith. *Boy of Old Prague.* Pantheon, 1963.

A graphic story of life in the Jewish ghetto in 1540 is told in this book.

Kent, Louise. *He Went with Drake.* Houghton, 1961.

This book recounts the adventures of young Oliver and his cousin, James, who sailed with Sir Frances Drake on the *Golden Hind.* They looked for sea routes and captured gold from Spanish vessels. Oliver became a spy for Drake and took part in the battle against the Armada in 1588.

McGraw, Eloise. *Master Cornhill.* Penguin, 1987.

Michael returns to London after being evacuated by his adoptive family during the plague but finds that not one of them has survived. His adventures, set in London in 1666, include the Great Fire of London and other events of the time.

Middleton, Haydn. *Everyday Life in the Sixteenth Century.* Silver Burdett, 1983.

Enormous wealth and terrible poverty, existing side by side, are described in this book.

Orczy, Baroness Emma. *The Scarlet Pimpernel.* Dell Yearling Classics, 1989.

This classic work of historical fiction, set during the French Revolution, is perhaps best read by advanced readers.

Schlesinger, Arthur. *Peter the Great: Russian Emperor.* Chelsea House, 1989.

The story of Peter the Great, the czar who was dedicated to the westernization of Russia, is told in this book.

Smith, Lacey. *Elizabeth Tudor: Biography of a Queen.* Little, Brown, 1977.

This book takes a chronological look at the diplomatic and political aspects of her reign and delves into the queen's character.

Sutcliff, Rosemary. *Bonnie Dundee.* Dutton, 1984.

The author weaves a tale of heroes, rogues, religious zealots, and soldiers who serve the king first; this is a story of conflict and war in seventeenth-century Scotland. See also *Flame-Colored Taffeta* by the same author.

Treviño, Elizabeth de. *I, Juan de Pareja.* Farrar, 1965.

Diego Velasquez inherits Juan de Pareja in the seventeenth century from a Seville relative. Juan learns to read and to paint in the service of Velasquez.

Turner, Dorothy. *Queen Elizabeth I.* Watts, 1987.

This is a chapter in the life of Queen Elizabeth, whose tiny navy defeated the 114 ships of the Spanish Armada.

Walsh, Jill Paton. *A Parcel of Patterns.* Farrar, 1983.

The time is 1665. A small English village is being decimated by the plague. Mall loses her loved ones but finds them again when the long ordeal is over.

Grade Eight:
U.S. History
and Geography—
Growth and Conflict

8.1   Connecting with Past Learnings: Our Colonial Heritage

Alderman, Clifford Lindsey. *The Story of the Thirteen Colonies.* Random, 1966.

Recently reprinted, this book devotes a chapter to each of the original colonies and provides historical background information. Because each chapter is essentially complete, the book lends itself to excerpting and use in preparing topical reports. Agriculture, economy, key figures, and ethnic heritage in the colonies are emphasized in the narrative.

Carse, Robert. *Early American Boats.* Illustrated by Hans Zander. World, 1968.

The fine line drawings and detailed text in this book describe the lively history of the wind- and oar-driven craft of early America during a period when the waterways were the only practical "roads" in North America.

Caselli, Giovanni. *The Renaissance and the New World.* Bedrick, 1986.

Everyday life in Europe and in the New World town of Jamestown, Virginia, is superbly illustrated with drawings of tools, weapons, and other artifacts of life from the fifteenth through the eighteenth centuries.

Daugherty, James. *The Landing of the Pilgrims.* Random, 1987.

Based on the journals of the Pilgrims, this book relates the history of the Plymouth settlers. Excerpts from primary documents are included.

Dillon, Ellis. *The Seekers.* Macmillan, 1986.

Sixteen-year-old Edward sails from England for the Pilgrims' colony after his beloved Rebecca is taken by her parents to the New World in 1632. This story is based on firsthand accounts of the period.

Douty, Esther. *Forten the Sailmaker: Pioneer Champion for Human Rights.* Rand McNally, 1968.

Forten lived during one of the most turbulent periods in American history, and he lived the life of a good American. A sailmaker and a free black man, he became one of the earliest American leaders in the battle for human rights.

Gray, Elizabeth Janet. *Penn.* Viking, 1938.

Gray is a scrupulous researcher and vivid writer. Her book deserves republication.

Kurelek, William. *They Sought a New World: The Story of European Immigration to North America.* Tundra Books, 1985.

Beautiful paintings and quotations from the writings of a gifted Canadian artist capture the richness and variety of the people who settled the North American continent.

Levitin, Sonia. *Roanoke: A Novel of the Lost Colony.* Atheneum, 1973.

This lively novel centers on a boy and his vain efforts to save the colony of Roanoke.

Meigs, Cornelia. *Master Simon's Garden.* Macmillan, 1916.

Three generations of a Puritan family, from colonial times to the early days of the new nation, are depicted in this book. Change and continuity are represented here with some appealing symbolism. Long-neglected and out of print, this book is still worth reading.

Mott, Michael. *Master Entrick.* Dell, 1986.

Young Robert Entrick is mysteriously kidnapped and forced to be a bond servant to a hard-bitten settler in eighteenth-century America during the French and Indian War. He befriends a young Indian, an act that changes his fortunes.

Speare, Elizabeth. *The Witch of Blackbird Pond.* Houghton, 1958.

An impetuous sixteen-year-old girl struggles against a Puritan community after being raised in free-thinking Barbados. She is accused of witchcraft after aiding an old woman. See also Speare's *Calico Captive,* a book based on an actual diary account of the French and Indian War.

Tunis, Edwin. *Colonial Craftsmen: The Beginnings of American Industry.* Crowell, 1965.

This book is a treasure for reviewing early American handicraft, manufacturing, commerce, and agricultural implements. See Tunis's *Colonial Living* and *Frontier Living* as well.

8.2 Connecting with Past Learnings: A New Nation

Alexander, Lloyd. *Westmark.* Dutton, 1981.

A young printer's apprentice is arrested with his master for printing seditious pamphlets during the revolutionary period in America.

Book of Great American Documents. Edited by Vincent Wilson, Jr. American History Research Associates, 1987.

This teacher's resource is an impressive collection of primary sources. See also Wilson's *Book of Distinguished American Women* and *Book of the Founding Fathers.*

Boorstin, Daniel J. *The Landmark History of the American People.* In two volumes. Random, 1987.

A renowned historian, Boorstin published this highly readable work for young readers in the 1960s. It has been updated and revised with new material on technological advances. Boorstin has a remarkable ability to make history an adventure.

Brand, Oscar. *Songs of '76: A Folksinger's History of the Revolution.* Evans, 1988.

This is a superb collection of songs collected from old manuscripts, newspapers, and hundreds of accounts. More than 60 songs, accompanied by history commentaries, make this a most valuable book.

Caudill, Rebecca. *Tree of Freedom.* Puffin (Penguin), 1988.

In every generation, the tree of freedom must be nurtured if it is to survive. This moving novel of family life is back in print.

Collier, James Lincoln, and Christopher Collier. *The Bloody Country.* Scholastic, 1985.

An ordinary Pennsylvania family struggling to make a home is again faced with the frightening prospect of war. The family may lose everything, including a friend who is half black and half Indian. This is an intense story of a fateful period of American history. See also *The Winter Hero* by the same author.

Edmonds, Walter. *Drums Along the Mohawk.* Little, Buccaneer, or Bantam paperbacks, various dates.

This epic novel of courageous pioneers of the Mohawk Valley during the revolutionary war is for advanced readers.

Forman, James. *The Cow Neck Rebels.* Farrar, 1969.

Bruce and Malcolm Cameron march off to the Battle of Long Island in August, 1776. The war tragically changes the futures of these two boys.

Fritz, Jean. *Early Thunder.* Putnam, 1967.

Fourteen-year-old Daniel is forced to choose between his pacifist family's Tory sympathies and his own feelings about Parliament's harsh response to the Boston Tea Party. The story is set in Salem, Massachusetts, in 1775. See also *Traitor, The Case of Benedict Arnold* by the same author.

Long, Hamilton Abert. *The American Ideal of 1776: The Twelve Basic American Principles.* Your Heritage Books, 1976.

In a discussion of our nation's founding and our democratic institutions, rooted as they are in Judeo-Christian religious thinking and English parliamentary traditions, this well-documented book builds its case. It offers helpful background for teachers; quotations from numerous primary sources are included. The book is handled in California by Telefact Foundation.

McPhillips, Martin. *The Battle of Trenton.* Silver Burdett, 1989.

With clear text amplified by excellent drawings, portraits, paintings, and quotations from Thomas Paine's *Common Sense,* this book describes the crisis leading to rebellion, the Battle of Trenton, and the victory that saved the cause of independence.

Marrin, Albert. *The War for Independence: The Story of the American Revolution.* Atheneum, 1988.

This is a carefully researched account of the revolutionary war period that includes well-grounded judgments about such key personalities as George Washington and Thomas Paine. It is illustrated with prints, paintings, and maps of the time.

Morris, Richard. *The Founding of the Republic.* Lerner, 1985.

This book is about a group of remarkable men whose heroic efforts made the experiment of the American republic a success.

O'Dell, Scott. *Sarah Bishop.* Houghton, 1980.

Fifteen-year-old Sarah Bishop is left without a surviving member of her family at the time of the American Revolution. Her father had remained loyal to the king, while her brother had joined the rebels. Then her possessions are destroyed in a raid, and Sarah is forced to find a new life on her own.

Paine, Thomas. *Common Sense.* Penguin, 1982.

An extensive introduction describes the background of the American Revolution and the life, career, and ideology of Thomas Paine.

Patriotic and Historical Plays for Young People. Edited by Sylvia Kamerman. Plays, 1987.

A collection of royalty-free plays, choral readings, and programs about the people and events that made America, this book is also usable at the fifth-grade level.

Rinaldi, Ann. *Time Enough for Drums.* Holiday, 1986.

Set during the War of Independence in New Jersey, this is the story of a young girl who experiences a family divided between loyalists and patriots.

8.3 The Constitution of the United States

Anderson, Joan. *1787.* Harcourt, 1987.

The college-age nephew of Thomas Mifflin, who is a delegate to the Constitutional Convention, is hired to assist James Madison in the writing of the Constitution. This work is light, recreational reading that is tinged with romance.

Ayars, James. *We Hold These Truths: From the Magna Carta to the Bill of Rights.* Viking, 1977.

This brief history of the ideas of liberty and equality contains sketches of the lives of Stephen Langton, John Lilburne, and George Mason, men who contributed to the development and preservation of these ideas. This book is appropriate for the mature reader.

Banfield, Susan. *James Madison.* Watts, 1986.

The story of the fourth President, who is often known as the Father of the Constitution, is recounted in this book.

Brill, Marlene Targ. *John Adams.* Children's Press, 1986.

Brill's work is a biography of the outspoken, decisive man who served his country in many ways.

Commager, Henry Steele. *The Great Constitution: A Book for Young Americans.* Eastern Acorn Press, 1982.

This paperback is an excellent candidate for classroom and students' use. Primary source material abounds, and the format is congenial in its presentation of the personalities and conflicts that shaped our founding document.

Díaz Cubero, José H. *Historia del Pueblo de los Estados Unidos de América.* Madrid: Compañía Cultural Editora y Distribuidora de Textos Americanos, 1989.

This Spanish-language history of the United States includes the text of the Constitution and the Bill of Rights. It is illustrated with photographs from the Bettman Archives.

Findlay, Bruce, and Esther Findlay. *Your Rugged Constitution.* Stanford University Press, 1969.

The unusual format of this out-of-print book makes studying the Constitution a somewhat simpler task.

Fisher, Dorothy Canfield. *Our Independence and the Constitution.* Random, Landmark reprint, 1964.

Through the eyes of one Philadelphia family, the reader relives the writing of the Declaration of Independence and the Constitution.

Hauptly, Denis J. *A Convention of Delegates: The Creation of the Constitution.* Atheneum, 1987.

This look at the creative process behind the writing of the U.S. Constitution is for mature readers.

Hilton, Suzanne. *We the People: The Way We Were, 1783–1793.* Westminster Press, 1981.

This book covers amusements, marriage, fashions, housekeeping, schools, government, fires, and everyday life after independence was achieved.

Kleeburg, Irene. *Separation of Church and State.* Watts, 1986.

Photographs and paintings illustrate this explanation of an important constitutional principle.

McPhillips, Martin. *The Constitutional Convention.* Silver Burdett, 1986.

This book traces the origins of this remarkable document to the Magna Charta. It continues with an introduction to the convention delegates and an explanation of the events that resulted in the Constitution. Good visuals are included.

Morris, Richard. *The Constitution* (Revised edition). Lerner, 1985.

This slim volume, written by a noted authority, contains much basic information on its subject. Other titles in this AMERICAN FOUNDING series also are worthwhile.

Quigley, Charles. *We the People* (middle grades version). Center for Civic Education, 1988.

The Constitution is examined in both its historical and contemporary settings in this book. Lessons are developed using cooperative learning strategies across six different topic areas. Teacher's and student's versions are available.

Sgroi, Peter. *This Constitution.* Watts, 1986.

The history of the Constitution, from its stormy development at the Constitutional Convention to its adoption and implementation as the law of the land, is described in this book.

Sliker, Harold G. *Our Heritage.* Samuel French, 1941.

Though slightly dated, this choric pageant can be a powerful tribute to the Bill of Rights when well presented. This royalty-free play is suitable for classroom reading or for use in a readers' theater.

8.4 Launching the Ship of State

Blassingame, Wyatt. *The Look-It-Up Book of Presidents.* Random, 1990.

This reference work contains concise biographical portraits of presidents studied in this unit. Other articles lend themselves to later units.

Broadman, F. W. *America and the Virginia Dynasty.* Walck, 1974.

This book covers the 20 continuous years during which Virginians were presidents of the United States.

Buehr, Walter. *1812: The War and the World.* Rand McNally, 1967.

This book puts the War of 1812 into a global perspective.

Cabral, Olga. *So Proudly She Sailed.* Houghton, 1981.

A fictionalized account of the U.S.S. *Constitution,* lovingly nicknamed Old Ironsides by her crew, from her launching in 1797 through her many battles and final restoration more than 100 years later.

Cooper, James Fenimore. *The Last of the Mohicans.* Scribner, 1986.

Back in print, this edition has compelling illustrations by N. C. Wyeth. Teachers may select excerpts from this or other LEATHERSTOCKING TALES, all of which are available in paperbound editions. SM (Colección Ballena Blanca) publishes a Spanish version with helpful notes and color illustrations.

Fleischman, Paul. *Path of the Pale Horse.* Harper, 1983.

Set in 1793, this is the story of a fourteen-year-old apprentice to a doctor during the yellow fever epidemic in Philadelphia that killed 10 percent of the population.

Fritz, Jean. *Great Little Madison.* Putnam, 1989.

Fritz's latest biography, this one tells of the life of one of the new nation's chief architects.

George Washington: A Collection. Edited by W. B. Allen. Liberty Press, 1988.

This teacher's resource of primary sources is a compendium of Washington's letters and speeches, and it can be used at the fifth grade level as well. Excerpts can be useful.

Gerson, Noel B. *Mr. Madison's War: The Second War for Independence.* Messner, 1967.

The War of 1812 is viewed from different perspectives, depending on positions of support or nonsupport.

Glubok, Shirley. *The Art of the New American Nation.* Macmillan, 1972.

This unusual book is a varied collection of visual art from 1776 to 1826. The commentary is easy to read and helps students to understand better the American culture of this era.

Irving, Washington. "Old Christmas," in *The Sketch Book.* Sleepy Hollow Press reprint, 1981. (Distributed by Fordham University Press.)

This story is excerpted from *The Sketch Book,* all of which is worthwhile reading. *Rip Van Winkle and The Legend of Sleepy Hollow* (one volume, Fordham) is also worth having. Washington Square Press issues a paperback, *Legend of Sleepy Hollow and Other Selections from Washington Irving,* edited by Austin M. Fox.

Leckie, Robert. *The War Nobody Won: 1812.* Putnam, 1974.

A divided nation and weak government were swept into a war for which they were totally unprepared. This is a dramatic story of heroes and villains put in a situation in which there was no winner.

Meltzer, Milton. *George Washington and the Birth of Our Nation.* Watts, 1986.

This book holds a wealth of fascinating factual content that focuses on Washington's adult life. This biography of the first President contains well-selected journal excerpts, drawings, and primary source material that includes Washington's notes for a draft of the U.S. Constitution.

Patterson, Charles. *Thomas Jefferson.* Watts, 1987.

In this book, Jefferson is presented in all his roles: politician, statesman, scientist, philosopher, and architect. David Adler's *Thomas Jefferson* is shorter and more easily read.

Tunis, Edwin. *The Young U.S.: 1783 to 1830.* Crowell, 1976.

The United States following the Revolution is described in this book. Included are accounts of personal and family life as well as important historical events. Also included are 165 detailed and accurate pencil drawings.

8.5 The Divergent Paths of the American People (1800–1850)

8.5.1 The West

Baker, Betty. *The Dunderhead War.* Harper, 1967.

Quincy and his father live in Independence, Missouri, in 1846. When the first news of the Mexican War comes, Quincy wants to volunteer but is too young.

Blos, Joan. *Brothers of the Heart.* Scribner, 1985.

From the author of *A Gathering of Days,* this suspenseful story is set in the Michigan wilderness during the 1800s. A young handicapped boy learns survival skills and self-esteem from an Indian woman.

Bohner, Charles. *Bold Journey: West with Lewis and Clark.* Houghton, 1985.

A fictionalized account of Private Hugh McNeal, a member of the Lewis and Clark expedition, this vivid novel captures the spirit of a young man's journey into the dangerous unknown and his meeting with native Americans.

Carey, Helen, and Judith E. Greenberg. *How to Use Primary Resources.* Watts, 1983.

This book offers helpful ideas for locating, developing, and interpreting primary source material.

Clifford, Eth. *The Year of the Three-Legged Deer.* Dell, 1973.

As a young man, Takawsu, half Leni-Lenape, comes to visit his white father, Jesse Benton. An attack on the Leni-Lenape by white men convinces Jesse's

Indian wife and son to join her tribe during the mass removal of Indians to western lands.

Cordier, Mary Hurlbut, and Maria A. Perez-Stable. *Peoples of the American West.* Scarecrow Press, 1989.

This teacher's and library resource is an annotated bibliography of more than 100 children's literature books that deal with settlement of lands west of the Mississippi.

Cwiklik, Robert. *Sequoyah and the Cherokee Alphabet.* Silver Burdett, 1989.

This well-told story of the lame Cherokee craftsman culminates in the "trail of tears."

Foster, Genevieve. *Andrew Jackson.* Scribner, 1951.

Jackson seemed to be always fighting: with other boys, against Indians or the Spanish, for the presidency, or for his laws.

Frazier, Neta. *Stout Hearted Seven: The True Adventure of the Sager Children Orphaned on the Oregon Trail in 1844.* Harcourt, 1973.

Thoroughly researched and based on the Whitman massacre, this fiction-on-fact work reads well and maintains students' interest. It is worthy of republication.

The Journals of Lewis and Clark: A New Selection. Edited by John Bakeless. New American Library (Mentor paperback), 1964.

This teacher's resource contains primary source material about the famous expedition. Excerpts can be useful.

Kherdian, David. *Bridger: The Story of a Mountain Man.* Greenwillow, 1987.

This is a diarylike account of Jim Bridger, the legendary scout and adventurer who first discovered the Great Salt Lake. Bridger relates his experiences over the years from 1822 through 1824. Good geographical material is included.

L'Amour, Louis. *How the West Was Won.* Thorndike Press, 1988.

L'Amour is best known as a storyteller and as a meticulous researcher of historical detail. This popular novel presents one more perspective of the westward movement. See also the Sackett novels by the same author.

Lawson, Don. *The United States in the Mexican War.* Illustrated by Robert F. McCullough. Harper, 1976.

"Mr. Polk's War" was not a popular one. President James K. Polk wanted to expand America's borders to include Texas, California, and New Mexico. Many citizens and politicians felt that the benefits of such an expansion would not justify a costly, bloody war. An account of the fall of the Alamo in 1836 is included.

McCall, Edith. *Message from the Mountains.* Walker, 1985.

Jim Mathews is fifteen years of age in 1826 in Franklin, Missouri, the town that was the eastern end of a trail that went to Santa Fe. This is a story of Jim and his friend Kit Carson.

McGraw, Eloise. *Moccasin Trail.* Penguin, 1986.

In 1854 an eighteen-year-old boy recalls the bear mauling that led him to live six years with the Crow Indians.

Murrow, Liza Ketchum. *West Against the Wind.* Holiday, 1987.

This first novel by a new author is set in the American frontier as a family travels west.

Noble, Iris. *Courage in Her Hands.* Messner, 1968.

Melinda is a sheltered sixteen-year-old taken in 1815 by her father from her small New England world to the strange new world of the Russian fur-trading colony at Fort Ross, California.

Ochoa, George. *The Fall of Mexico City.* Silver Burdett, 1989.

This is a concise, attractively illustrated presentation of the Mexican-American War.

Phelan, Mary Kay. *The Story of the Louisiana Purchase.* Crowell, 1979.

Drawing on journals, letters, and other firsthand accounts, Phelan recreates the everyday life of New Orleans and the American frontier, as well as the long, secret negotiations for the purchase in Paris. The writer also portrays the historical figures who played significant parts in this pivotal event in American history.

Rourke, Constance. *Davy Crockett*. Harcourt, 1934.

Rourke carefully researched fact and fiction surrounding this American figure. She tells Crockett's story, drawing from his personal writings as a primary source. Her book deserves republication.

Soul of America, Documenting Our Past, 1492–1974. Edited by Robert C. Baron. Fulcrum, Inc., 1989.

More than 100 speeches and documents from U.S. history are contained in this helpful resource of primary documents.

Taylor, Theodore. *Walking Up a Rainbow*. Delacorte, 1986.

Susan Carlisle, a feisty, courageous, fourteen-year-old Iowa orphan, embarks in 1852 on a daring and somewhat foolish venture. Taylor's plot takes Susan on a cross-country journey full of hardship, adventure, danger, and a little romance.

Tocqueville, Alexis de. *Democracy in America*. Edited by Phillips Bradley. Random, 1944.

These two paperbound volumes are useful as a teacher's background publication. Excerpts are possible.

Turner, Ann. *Third Girl from the Left*. Macmillan, 1986.

Itching to do something different, eighteen-year-old Sarah leaves Maine for the harsh Montana environment as a mail-order bride and is soon left a widow with a 2,000-acre (809.7 hectares) ranch to run.

Vance, Marguerite. *The Jacksons of Tennessee*. Dutton, 1953.

The fated marriage of Rachel and Andrew Jackson is portrayed in this book. It is worthy of republication.

8.5.2 The Northeast

Blos, Joan. *A Gathering of Days: A New England Girl's Journal, 1830–32*. Macmillan, 1982.

Thirteen-year-old Catherine Hall keeps a journal of her last year on a New Hampshire farm where she keeps house for her widowed father. The journal

shows her kindness and determination and the maturity she gains as she learns to cope with increased responsibilities.

Cooper, Ilene. *Susan B. Anthony*. Watts, 1984.

This is a biography of the great American proponent of women's rights.

Dickens, Charles. *American Notes for General Circulation*. St. Martin or Penguin, various dates.

The youthful, rough America of 1842 is vividly recalled in this journal of Dickens's famous tour of the country.

Jacobs, William Jay. *Mother, Aunt Susan and Me*. Coward, 1979.

This readable account of Susan B. Anthony's and Elizabeth Cady Stanton's efforts to win equal rights for women was written from the point of view of Stanton's sixteen-year-old daughter, Harriet. It is a story of courage and dignity.

Levinson, Nancy Smiler. *The First Women Who Spoke Out*. National Women's History Project. Dillon, 1983.

This book is valuable in tracing the development of the women's rights movement.

Macaulay, David. *Mill*. Houghton, 1983.

Macaulay has distinguished himself through his illustrations, readable text, and design. In this work he presents mills as they would have looked in New England in the 1800s. His book is useful for any study of industry in the nineteeth century.

Rothe, Bertha. *Daniel Webster Reader*. Oceana Publications, 1965.

Currently, Daniel Webster's writings are available only in costly, scholarly editions. This book provides at least a sampling of his work; it is available in paperback.

Selden, Bernice. *The Mill Girls: Lucy Larcom, Harriet Hanson Robinson, and Sarah G. Bagley*. Atheneum, 1983.

In this useful teacher's resource, the lives of women who worked in the mills at Lowell, Massachusetts, reflect the effects of industrialization on New England during this period.

8.5.3 The South

Barnard, Jacqueline. *Journey Toward Freedom.* Norton, 1967.

> This is the story of the black slave woman who grew up to champion the rights of blacks, women, and labor.

Burchard, Peter. *Bimby.* Coward, 1968.

> The story is told of the day of decision in the life of a young slave in the Sea Islands off Georgia before the Civil War.

Claflin, Edward Beecher. *Sojourner Truth and the Struggle for Freedom.* BARRON'S EDUCATIONAL SERIES (Children's Press, distributor), 1987.

> An engrossing, inspiring account of "a woman venerable for age, distinguished for insight . . . remarkable for independence and courageous self-assertion."

Douglass, Frederick. *The Life and Times of Frederick Douglass.* Macmillan, 1962.

> The story of a true American hero is told in his own words. Douglass speaks of his race and for all humanity. See also Douglass's *The Narrative and Selected Writings* (Modern Library, 1981).

Faber, Doris. *I Will Be Heard: The Life of William Lloyd Garrison.* Lothrop, 1970.

> This book sketches the life of the American abolitionist who began his campaign against the evils of slavery 30 years before the Civil War.

Fox, Paula. *The Slave Dancer.* Bradbury, 1973.

> The story is told in this book of Jessie Miller, a thirteen-year-old boy in 1840, who is kidnapped and spends four months on a slave ship playing music to make the slaves dance.

Franklin, John Hope. *From Slavery to Freedom.* Random, 1967.

> This history is written by a scholar who has been deemed the dean of Afro-American historians.

Hamilton, Virginia. *Anthony Burns: The Defeat and Triumph of a Fugitive Slave.* Knopf, 1988.

> This is the story of a twenty-year-old slave who fled from Virginia to Boston in 1854. It tells of his arrest and trial and his struggle to maintain his faith in humanity.

Kemble, Fanny. *Description of Life on a Southern Plantation.*

> No suitable edition of this primary source is in print except as a part of expensive, scholarly editions. Some libraries may stock anthologies that contain excerpts. This book is recommended in the *History–Social Science Framework for California Public Schools, Kindergarten Through Grade Eight.*

Lester, Julius. *To Be a Slave.* Dial Books, 1968.

> This book provides a re-creation of an actual happening in the early years of this nation. See also *Long Journey Home* by the same author.

Reit, Seymour. *Behind Rebel Lines: The Incredible Story of Emma Edmonds, Civil War Spy.* Harcourt, 1988.

> Emma Edmonds was a soldier, spy, and nurse who first fought in the Union army and then served as a spy while working in Confederate field hospitals. Throughout the war, she posed as a man and struggled to keep her identity and sex a secret.

Smucker, Barbara. *Runaway to Freedom.* Harper, 1979.

> This novel, based on the underground railway, is written from a Canadian's viewpoint. Authentic, firsthand accounts were used in forming the story.

Stowe, Harriet Beecher. *Uncle Tom's Cabin.* Bantam, 1981.

> This is a work of tremendous historical importance. The illustrations add another dimension to this vision of the Old South before the Civil War. George L. Aiken's dramatized version (Samuel French, publisher) toured the nation throughout the late 1800s and is worth investigating. A Spanish version of the novel is published in Madrid by SM (Colección Ballena Blanca).

Walker, David, and Henry H. Garnet. *Walker's Appeal and Garnet's Address to the Slaves of the United States of America.* Ayer, 1969.

> These works by Walker and Garnet are two vivid primary sources for this unit.

8.6   Toward a More Perfect Union: 1850–1879

Abraham Lincoln. Holt (Caminos Abiertos), n.d.

This is a Spanish-language biography of the Great Emancipator.

Alcott, Louisa May. *Little Women.* Little, Brown, 1968.

This is the classic story of the March family whose members experience the harshness of poverty and the hard lessons of growing up in New England during the Civil War. A Spanish version is published by Everest, Aguilar, and other publishers. Little, Brown issues Alcott's entire series in its ORCHARD HOUSE editions.

Angle, Paul. *A Pictorial History of the Civil War Years.* Doubleday, 1980.

Recently issued in paperback, this book is a trove of valuable photographic material. Angle, a respected historian, presents an engaging narrative for eighth grade readers.

Beatty, Patricia. *Charley Skedaddle.* Morrow, 1987.

Charley, a rough twelve-year-old boy from a Bowery gang, enlists as a drummer boy in the Union army to avenge his older brother's death at Gettysburg. Later, he deserts from the battlefield. Through several events that test his mettle, Charley develops into a brave young man. See also *Be Ever Hopeful, Hannalee* by the same author.

Camus, William. *Azules Contra Grises.* Madrid: SM (El Barco de Vapor, Serie Roja), n.d.

This Spanish-language work of historical fiction deals with the American Civil War.

Clapp, Patricia. *The Tamarack Tree.* Lothrop, 1986.

This is a first-person account of the siege of Vicksburg, Mississippi, written by a teenage British girl. The girl feels the North is right but feels grief over her friendships in the South.

Coffey, Vincent J. *The Battle of Gettysburg.* Silver Burdett, 1985.

Illustrated with paintings, maps, photographs, and

portraits, this title presents the events of the Civil War that led to the Battle of Gettysburg and describes the battle and its aftermath.

Coit, Margaret L. *The Fight for Union.* Houghton, 1961.

The brilliant opposition of intellects and personalities in the years preceding the Civil War is dramatically shown during a time when slavery—its morality and its economics—became the burning issue in the United States.

Fahrmann, Willi. *The Long Journey of Lucas B.* Bradbury Press, 1985.

A young boy leaves Europe for America in search of his father. Geography, transportation, and Prussian settlements are faithfully depicted in this novel set at the time of the Reconstruction.

Freedman, Russell. *Lincoln: A Photobiography.* Clarion, 1987.

This biography, filled with photographs, delineates the issues of Lincoln's day as well as his life.

Fritz, Jean. *Brady.* Penguin, 1987.

Brady accidentally discovers the Underground Railroad station in his small Pennsylvania town, is confused by his father's denial, and then endangers the effort because he cannot keep his mouth shut.

Haley, Alex. *A Different Kind of Christmas.* Doubleday, 1988.

This novel weaves a Christmas season story that is set in 1855 amidst conditions that affected the Underground Railroad.

Hansen, Joyce. *Out from This Place.* Walker, 1988.

The Civil War and the Reconstruction period presented unique challenges to ex-slaves. This book helps readers understand the hardships and appreciate the inner resourcefulness of the newly freed population. See also *Which Way Freedom?* by the same author.

Hayman, Leroy. *The Death of Lincoln: A Picture History of the Assassination.* Scholastic, 1987.

A fascinating, well-researched history of the assassination, this book reinforces students' learning about the Civil War. Photographs and sketches of the era are included.

Hunt, Irene. *Across Five Aprils.* Berkley, 1987.

The Creighton family becomes involved in the Civil War in April, 1861, on their farm in Illinois. This story tells how each family member was affected.

Hurmence, Belinda. *Tancy.* Clarion, 1984.

Characterization and historical detail are incorporated into this Civil War tale. Tancy, a young slave girl, is freed, discovers the meaning of freedom, and realizes the danger of illusions during her search for identity.

Johnson, Neil. *The Battle of Gettysburg.* Four Winds, 1989.

This narrative is accompanied by black-and-white photographs of the 1988 reenactment. The book contains the full text of Lincoln's Gettysburg Address.

Kantor, MacKinlay. *Gettysburg.* Random, 1963.

History comes alive in this engrossing, easily read account written by a distinguished American author.

Kassem, Lou. *Listen for Rachel.* McElderry (Macmillan), 1986.

This is an American Civil War story based on the Appalachian legend that if one hears hoofbeats, Miss Rachel is riding to tend the sick.

Keith, Harold. *Rifles for Watie.* Harper, 1987.

A boy who longs to be in the Union army discovers the cruelty and savagery that war brings out in some men. This tale is set in Kansas during the Civil War.

Lincoln, Abraham. "Gettysburg Address," in *Favorite Poems, Old and New.* Edited by Helen Ferris. Doubleday, 1957.

This collection also contains John Greenleaf Whittier's "Barbara Frietchie," Nancy Byrd Turner's "Lincoln," and Henry Wadsworth Longfellow's "Sail On, O Ship of State."

Meltzer, Milton. *Voices from the Civil War.* Crowell, 1989.

The author describes this collection of primary source materials as a "documentary history" of the Civil War. The reader is given a background sketch of each individual who is quoted. See also *The Black*

Americans: A History in Their Own Words (Crowell, 1987).

Monjo, F. N. *Me and Willie and Pa.* Simon and Schuster, 1973.

The story of Abraham Lincoln is told in this book from the viewpoint of his son, Tad. See also *Vicksburg Veteran.*

North, Sterling. *Abe Lincoln: Log Cabin to White House.* Random, 1963.

This LANDMARK SERIES reprint emphasizes the period prior to Lincoln's White House years. The political challenges Lincoln faced and the strategies he used to gain positions of leadership are among the areas that are highlighted.

O'Dell, Scott. *The 290.* Houghton, 1976.

The dramatic story of a boy and one of the most famous vessels of the Civil War is told in this book.

Perez, N. A. *The Slopes of War.* Houghton, 1984.

This panoramic novel brings to life the men who fought at Gettysburg and the people of Gettysburg, who watched brother fight brother and then had to cope with the aftermath of that terrible battle.

Petry, Ann. *Harriet Tubman: Conductor on the Underground Railroad.* Harper, 1955.

A sensitive account is given here of the woman who led more than 300 black fugitives to freedom through the Underground Railroad.

Steele, William. *The Perilous Road.* Harcourt, 1958.

A Tennessee mountain boy who hates the Yankees learns the real meaning of war when his older brother joins the Union army.

Stone, Melissa. *Clouds of War.* Steck-Vaughn, 1989.

Written for lower-level readers, this book features six biographical portraits of notable Civil War figures. It is one of the *MOMENTS IN AMERICAN HISTORY* series.

Weidhorn, Manfred. *Robert E. Lee.* Atheneum, 1988.

A balanced and admiring portrait of this Confederate military hero.

Wisler, G. Clifton. *Thunder on the Tennessee.* Lodestar, 1983.

 A Texas boy enlists as a Confederate soldier and learns the gritty and ugly reality of war.

8.7 The Rise of Industrial America: 1877–1914

Aldrich, Bess Streeter. *A Lantern in Her Hand.* Signet paperback or Amereon House reprint, various dates.

 Solid writing and warm characterization make this an engaging story of Nebraska pioneers. The entire life of its strong female protagonist is covered in a story that bridges the pioneer and industrial periods. The prolific Aldrich is currently receiving revived interest.

Alger, Horatio. *Jed, The Poorhouse Boy.* Amereon House reprint, 1976.

 No understanding of the industrial era is complete without a glimpse of Alger's rags-to-riches heroes. Alger is often referred to in contemporary articles and essays, and his work reflects the values (and prejudices) of his time. Penguin has issued a paperback containing both *Ragged Dick* and *Struggling Upward* by the same author.

Bailey, Thomas A., and David M. Kennedy. *The American Spirit.* Vol. 1 and 2. Heath, 1987.

 This teacher's resource, best suited for more advanced readers, is a collection of primary sources containing usable material for the eighth grade; e.g., statements by Ulysses S. Grant, Booker T. Washington, and Chief Joseph. Volume 1 appears in the fifth-grade listings.

Beatty, Patricia. *Turn Homeward, Hannalee.* Morrow, 1984.

 Georgia mill workers are branded traitors to the Union and transported north so that their skills cannot be used by the Confederacy. This book shows the effects of the war on non–slave-owning working class people who fought for the Confederacy because they felt themselves to be Southerners.

Benet, Stephen Vincent. *The Ballad of William Sycamore.* Little, Brown, 1972.

 This soulful ballad tells of a rugged pioneer whose sons die at the Alamo and with General George Custer. Sycamore endures to old age and expires just as the nation's cities begin to spread across the land. Brinton Turkle's illustrations make this a priority for republication.

Bowman, John S. *Andrew Carnegie: Steel Tycoon.* Silver Burdett, 1989.

 This is the remarkable story of a Scottish immigrant's rise to wealth. The expansion and industrial development of the United States are shown, as well as Carnegie's later philanthropy. The work is one of Silver Burdett's THE AMERICAN DREAM series.

Boylston, Helen Dore. *Clara Barton: Founder of the American Red Cross.* Random, 1983.

 At the start of the Civil War, the United States had no trained nurses. This biography discusses Barton's work during and after the Civil War. She lived until 1912, and her life was a career of service and sacrifice.

Brown, Dee. *Lonesome Whistle: The Story of the First Transcontinental Railroad.* Adapted by Linda Proctor. Holt, 1980.

 In 1869 the last spike needed to complete the first transcontinental railroad linking the East and West coasts was pounded into place. The story that leads up to the placement of this last spike is filled with adventure, frustration, corruption, and success. This book describes how the railroad began, how it was built with the labor of immigrants, how it was plagued by outlaws, and how it helped destroy the lands of the Indian tribes.

Cather, Willa. *My Antonia.* Houghton, 1962.

 A Czech family living in a prairie town in Nebraska struggles with unfavorable economic conditions. The story centers on Antonia, a quiet and industrious young girl who later becomes a mother herself. It is Antonia's strength and her pioneer integrity that maintain those around her. Written with sympathy and power, it is a vivid, loving portrayal of an immigrant pioneer family and its members' assimilation into American ways.

Clemens, Samuel. *The Adventures of Huckleberry Finn.* Various editions.

 Mark Twain's American classic is filled with humor and insight. See also Twain's *Life on the Mississippi* (portions can be extracted). Spanish-language versions of *Huck Finn* and *Tom Sawyer* are published by Everest.

Coffey, Ellen Greenman. *John D. Rockefeller.* Silver Burdett, 1989.

This biography of "the pious robber baron" helps to link the study of nineteenth-century industrial America with the present.

Conrad, Pamela. *Prairie Songs.* Harper, 1985.

Contrasts of the barren Nebraska prairie—beauty and peace to some; loneliness and madness to others—are presented in this book. In a grim ending, a young doctor's wife goes mad when her baby is stillborn.

Cousins, Margaret. *The Story of Thomas Alva Edison.* Random, 1965.

Cousins's biography of the great inventor is one of the books in the *Landmark Series* now being reissued in paperback. Authentic photographs, sketches, and diagrams illustrate the text in a clear and helpful fashion.

Davis, Russell. *Chief Joseph: War Chief of the Nez Perce.* McGraw, 1962.

This book tells the saga of the renowned warrior and recounts the long, bitter struggle over settlement and control of the West.

Dunbar, Paul Laurence. *Complete Poems of Paul Laurence Dunbar.* Dodd, Mead, 1980.

Though recently out of print, this collection is still usable in both history–social science and English–language arts classes. Dunbar is one of the outstanding poets of our Afro-American heritage. Various publishers, such as Ayer, AMS, and Greenwood, reprint numerous single volumes of Dunbar's work, which schools may consider purchasing (e.g., *Poems of Cabin and Field, Joggin' erlong,* and *Lyrics of Sunshine and Shadow*).

Ellis, K. *Thomas Edison, Genio de la Electricidad.* n.p. Adara (Pioneros de la C. y D.), n.d.

This is a Spanish-language biography of the great inventor. See also Juan Ignacio Herrera's biography of the same name (Spain: Susaeta, 1981).

Force, Eden. *Theodore Roosevelt.* Watts, 1987.

This is a biography of the twenty-sixth President, who, among other achievements, transformed himself from a sickly youth into a hero of the Spanish-American War.

Freedman, Russell. *Buffalo Hunt.* Holiday, 1988.

A noteworthy blend of history and art is presented here by an author who is highly respected for his works. See also Freedman's *Children of the Wild West* (Ticknor and Fields, 1983).

Hilton, Suzanne. *The Way It Was—1876.* Westminster, 1975.

Details of everyday life in 1876 are detailed, revealing a time when the Industrial Revolution had just begun to change people's lives.

Hoxie, Frederick E. *The Crow.* Chelsea House, 1989.

A history of the Crow Indians of the Great Plains is presented here in chronological fashion. It includes the effects of white migration and settlement.

Hoyt, Harlowe R. *Town Hall Tonight!* Bramhall, 1961.

This book is out of print but is available in some public libraries. It is an excellent memoir of grassroots American cultural phenomena: the small town "opera house" and the itinerant theater company. Hoyt's excerpts from actual scripts and ads of the day give good examples of manners, mores, and theatrical styles. Good photographs are included. It can be used by teachers or students.

Kane, Harnett T. *Young Mark Twain and the Mississippi.* Random, *Landmark Series*, 1966.

This biography is drawn from Samuel Clemens's own recollections of a picturesque period in American history.

Katz, William. *Black Indians: A Hidden Heritage.* Atheneum, 1986.

Useful as a teacher's resource, Katz's book deals with a little-known aspect of U.S. history. The writer includes some controversies and provides a credible level of scholarship to this account.

Keith, Harold. *The Obstinate Land*. Crowell, 1977.

Fritz Romberg is thirteen years old when his family takes part in the Oklahoma land run in 1893. Ranchers resent the intrusion by the farmers, and crops are threatened or destroyed by weather. When Fritz's father dies in a blizzard, Fritz assumes the responsibility for the family.

Lens, Sidney. *Strikemakers and Strikebreakers*. Lodestar, 1985.

Strikes, lockouts, and the growth of unions come alive in this well-researched book on the history of the labor movement in the United States.

Levinson, Nancy Smiler. *I Lift My Lamp: Emma Lazarus and the Statue of Liberty*. Lodestar, 1986.

The framework strands of "national identity" and "cultural literacy" can be addressed through this biography. The narrative is detailed but interestingly told.

Loeper, John J. *Going to School in 1876*. Atheneum, 1984.

This study of school life complements this unit.

The Lowell Offering: Writings by New England Mill Women (1840–1845). Edited by Benita Eisler. Harper, 1980.

This anthology consists of letters, stories, and so forth written by the Lowell mill women. This material is for mature readers and should be used discriminately.

McGuffey, William Holmes, and others. MCGUFFEY'S ECLECTIC READERS. Mott Media or Van Nostrand Reinhold, reprinters, n.d.

These classic readers educated millions of Americans and tell us much about our history and ourselves. Mott's 1836 edition is modified; some material is deleted. The 1879 edition, the one remembered by most Americans, is sold by Van Nostrand Reinhold. Both are worth owning since the contents differ.

Miller, Marilyn. *The Transcontinental Railroad*. Silver Burdett, 1986.

Attractive photographs and maps illustrate the history of the railroad from the 1820s to the 1890s.

Pelta, Kathy. *Alexander Graham Bell*. Silver Burdett, 1989.

The life of the great inventor is interestingly told in this book. Bell's story is illustrated with authentic photographs and sketches of people, events, and early inventions.

Perez, N. A. *Breaker*. Houghton, 1988.

Set in a Pennsylvania coal-mining town at the turn of the century, this fictional account of fourteen-year-old Pat McFarlane's life as a slate picker is enriched with historical details about early labor organizing. It includes a portrait of prejudice toward immigrants who came to work the mines.

Pimlott, John. *The First World War*. Watts, 1986.

Profusely illustrated with authentic photographs, this book's concise discussion of the "Great War" is a good introduction to the topic. It includes America's entry into the catastrophe.

Reynolds, Quentin. *Custer's Last Stand*. Random, 1964.

A paperback reprint from the LANDMARK SERIES, this book is a good introduction to one of the most famous events in American history.

Rice, Alice Hegan. *Mrs. Wiggs of the Cabbage Patch*. Amereon, Ltd., n.d.

This short novel of charity and optimism in the midst of poverty provides insight into American mores and ethics at the turn of the century. The Cabbage Patch was an actual shantytown in Louisville, Kentucky; Rice lived nearby in the affluent St. James Court district. The story is based on Rice's philanthropic experiences; she was later honored by Eleanor Roosevelt for her writing and social concern. Paperback editions are available.

Riis, Jacob. *Children of the Tenements*. Ayer Co. reprint of 1903 edition.

Riis was a prolific chronicler of social conditions in the United States, and this work is representative of several that are currently in print. Useful excerpts can be drawn from the book.

Rolvaag, O. E. *Giants of the Earth*. Harper, 1965.

The hardships of Scandinavian settlers in the northern United States are depicted in this lengthy novel. Sections can be read aloud or extracted.

Shorto, Russell. *Geronimo and the Struggle for Apache Freedom.* Silver Burdett, 1989.

Several decades of American history are spanned in this book, which ends with Geronimo's death in 1912.

Skurzynski, Gloria. *The Tempering.* Clarion, 1983.

Set in a coal-mining town at the turn of the century, this novel presents the experiences of European immigrants.

Weitzman, David. *Windmills, Bridges, and Old Machines: Discovering Our Industrial Past.* Scribner, 1982.

This book explores America's industrial history and may incite students' interest in our industrial past. Especially noteworthy are diagrams of bridge construction and steam locomotives and descriptions of the operation of waterwheels, windmills, and canal locks.

Wiggin, Kate Douglas. *The Birds' Christmas Carol.* Houghton or Dell, various dates.

First published in the 1880s, this still-popular story is an example of the kind of sentiment contained in the better juvenile literature of the era.

Wilder, Laura Ingalls. *On the Way Home.* Harper, 1962.

Students who enjoyed works from the LITTLE HOUSE series in earlier grades will enjoy reading this personal journal of the Wilders' move to Mansfield, Missouri, in 1894.

8.8   Linking Past to Present

The American Reader, Words That Moved a Nation. Edited by Diane Ravitch. Harper Collins, 1990.

An annotated trove of essays, speeches, songs, and poems, this compendium offers a chronological arrangement of American heritage writings from the 1600s to the present. The collection reveals a variety of perspectives and experiences, all displaying the American spirit. Sufficient material is found here to supply teachers with primary sources, "core" literature, and supplementary reading materials. It is an indispensable teacher's resource.

Armstrong, William H. *Sounder.* Illustrated by James Barkley. Harper, 1969.

A sharecropper whose crops were poor and whose children were hungry steals a ham and some sausage. He is arrested, his hunting dog is nearly killed, and his family is left without him. This story reveals the racial injustices of the times.

Ashabranner, Brent. *Born to the Land: An American Portrait.* Putnam, 1989.

Farming and ranching families are central in this presentation of rural life in Luna County, New Mexico. It is illustrated with photographs. Ashabranner's *The New Americans* and *Always to Remember* also address contemporary aspects of national life.

Bales, Carol Ann. *Tales of the Elders: A Memory Book of Men and Women Who Came to America as Immigrants, 1900–1930.* Follett, 1977.

This is a collection of the stories of immigrants who came to America during the Great Migration seeking refuge from hunger and political turmoil.

Brown, Sterling A., et al., *The Negro Caravan.* Ayer, reprint of 1941 edition.

This valuable compendium of Afro-American literature is a cornucopia of poetry, short stories, plays, speeches, and essays. The comparative time line in the back is a noteworthy resource of historical information. The content of this book, first published in 1941, spans more than 100 years of literary heritage. The cost of this volume may be prohibitive for many schools.

Day, Carol Olsen, and Edmond Day. *The New Immigrants.* Watts, 1985.

This book describes the conditions of both the legal and illegal immigrants in the United States and examines the problems and controversies surrounding immigration today.

Fleming, Thomas. *Behind the Headlines.* Walker, 1989.

Change, civic values, and the Constitution are all reflected in this history of American newspapers. The author includes anecdotes of people and events.

Frank, Rudolph. *No Hero for the Kaiser.* Lothrop, 1986.

First written after World War I in Germany, this book tells how a Polish boy learns of the turmoil of tyranny in his country. This book was banned and burned in Nazi Germany.

Great American Stories, Poems and Essays. Compiled by Hugh Graham. Galahad Books, 1985.

First issued in 1949 by Spencer Press, this collection of patriotic writings contains a number of noteworthy pieces on traditional themes. Included are bits by Mark Twain and Washington Irving. William Cullen Bryant's "Freedom Never Sleeps" is short and worth discussion.

Greenfield, Eloise, and Lessie Jones Little. *Childtimes.* Crowell, 1979.

This is the memoir of three black women—grandmother, mother, and daughter.

Hanmer, Trudy. *The Growth of Cities.* Watts, 1985.

The growth of cities in America is traced in this book from colonial days to modern times, and the problems and promises of urbanization are discussed. See also Jane Jacobs's *Death and Life of Great American Cities*, a useful resource for teachers.

Hart, William. *The United States and World Trade.* Watts, 1985.

This book addresses the role of the United States in international economic matters and the effects of world trade on developing nations.

Hautzig, Esther. *The Endless Steppe.* Harper Junior, 1987.

Set in Poland and Siberia during World War II, this book is based on the author's childhood. Because it presents the harsh brutalities of a totalitarian regime, students can reflect on the purposes and benefits of freedom. This is a good book for use at the end of the year.

Horwitz, Elinor. *The Bird, the Banner and Uncle Sam.* Lippincott, 1976.

The story of patriotic symbols and images and the boundless imagination of craftspeople and artists is presented in this book by means of clear text and superb illustrations.

Jakoubek, Robert. *Martin Luther King, Jr.* Chelsea House, 1989.

Prints and black-and-white photographs illustrate this biography of the great civil rights leader. The book is one of a series on notable Afro-Americans.

Kendall, Martha E. *Elizabeth Cady Stanton.* Highland Publishing, 1988.

This paperback biography tells of the founder of the American women's rights movement. The narrative is engaging, using imaginary dialogue as a means of conveying Stanton's goals, ambitions, and achievements.

Kherdian, David. *The Road from Home: The Story of an Armenian Girl.* Greenwillow, 1979.

The oppression of Armenians by Turkey leads to an Armenian family's emigration to the United States.

L'Amour, Louis. *The Last of the Breed.* Bantam, 1980.

Set in the twentieth century, this novel tells of an American Indian taken prisoner by the Soviets. It addresses not only ethnicity but also heroism, self-reliance, and individualism.

McKissack, Patricia. *Jesse Jackson: A Biography.* Scholastic, 1989.

McKissack traces the Afro-American clergyman's rise to his present prominence as an advocate for blacks' causes and as a commanding speaker on the national scene.

Meltzer, Milton. *All Times, All Peoples: A World History of Slavery.* Harper, 1980.

This brief but powerful history helps students acquire a necessary perspective of this tragic condition. See also *The Chinese Americans* by the same author.

Poems of American History. Edited by Burton Stevenson. Ayer reprint, n.d.

Usable at more than one grade level, Stevenson's collection has long been a standard. Selections may be made to complement particular units.

Schaefer, Jack. *Shane.* Houghton, 1954.

A feud among Wyoming homesteaders in 1889 is the background for this dramatic character portrayal. Shane's influence on young Bob Starrett is one of the memorable features of this novel.

Sloane, Eric. ***Once Upon a Time: The Way America Was.*** Hastings, 1982.

A thoughtful, pointed look at America's devotion to handicrafts, wood, and frugality, with an admonition to preserve such endeavors and interests in our modern age.

Smith, Betsy Covington. ***Women Win the Vote.*** Silver Burdett, 1989.

A well-illustrated overview of the major figures and developments in the women's movement is provided in this book.

Stein, Conrad. ***The Story of the Nineteenth Amendment.*** Children's Press, 1982.

This is a brief, easy-to-read account of a milestone in women's rights.

Taylor, Mildred. ***Roll of Thunder, Hear My Cry.*** Dial, 1976.

This is a powerful novel of racism in the South, circa 1930. See also Taylor's *Let the Circle Be Unbroken.*

Wolf, Bernard. ***In This Proud Land: The Story of a Mexican-American Family.*** Lippincott, 1988.

One of the more recent works about migrant Mexicans who come to this country to work, this book depicts a close and loving family.

Zane, Polly, and John Zane. ***American Women: Four Centuries of Progress.*** The Proof Press, 1989.

This book contains much helpful information about significant persons and events. Sketch portraits of 24 prominent women in American history are sold with the book. It is a useful teacher's resource for this grade level.

Index of Authors

Index of Titles

Publishers and Distributors

Most of the publishers and distributors cited in this publication are based in the United States, and information on how to contact them is readily available in R. R. Bowker's *Books in Print,* which you can find in the majority of public libraries and bookstores.

Some of the United States publishers noted herein, however, are not included in *Books in Print.* Information for contacting them is listed below.

Also below are data on foreign publishers and distributors whose materials are described within. The list of foreign companies also includes several foreign language bookstores and distributors that might be able to help you find entries that are difficult to locate.

United States Publishers and Distributors Not Listed in *Books in Print*

Center for Civic Education
5414 Douglas Fir Road
Calabasas, CA 91302

Elementary-Secondary Education
Committee
Early Music America
30 W. Twenty-sixth Street,
Suite 1001
New York, NY 10010-2011

Photo Aids
P.O. Box 956
Mount Dora, FL 32757

Telefact Foundation
P.O. Box 1853
Sacramento, CA 95812

Women in the World
1030 Spruce Street
Berkeley, CA 94707

Spanish-Language Publishers

This list of Spanish-language publishers is arranged alphabetically by the shortened name for each company used in the text.

Alfaguara
Ediciones Alfaguara
Juan Bravo, 38
Madrid 28006, España
Telephone 800-526-0107

Altea
Ediciones Altea
Juan Bravo, 38 Apdo. 13166
Madrid 28006, España

Anaya
Ediciones Anaya
Irarte 3-4, Apdo. 14632
Madrid 28028, España
Telephone 91-246-76-00

Avance
Francisco Olejnik Alba Libros de
Chile
Puente 572-F
Santiago, Chile

Edaf
Ediciones y Distribuciones Edaf
Jorge Juan, 30
Madrid 28001, España

Ekaré
Ediciones Ekaré/Banco del Libro
Final Av. Luis Roche, Altamira
Sur Apdo. Postal 5893
Caracas 1010A, Venezuela
Telephone 323136/334322/
333110

Everest
Editorial Everest
Carretera León-La Coruña-Km. 5
Apdo. 339
León 24080, España
Telephone 987-23-59-04

Generales Anaya
Ediciones Generales Anaya
Villafranca 22
Madrid 28028, España

Juventud
Editorial Juventud
Provenza 101, Apdo. 3
Barcelona 08029, España

Juventud (U.S. distributor)
Libros Centroamericanos
P.O. Box 2203
Redlands, CA 92373
Telephone (714) 798-1342

Lumen
Lumen, Inc.
446 W. Twentieth Street
New York, NY 10011
Telephone (212) 989-7944

Nueva Imagen
Editorial Nueva Imagen
Escollo 316 Col. Las Aguilas, Del.
Alvaro Obregón
México 01710, D.F., México

Plaza y Janés
Editorial Plaza y Janés
Atn. Ignacio Fraile
Virgen de Guadalupe 21-23
Esplugues de Llobregat
Barcelona, España

SM
Ediciones SM
  c/o Joaquín Turina 39
  Madrid 28044, España
  Telephone 208-51-45

Timún Más
Editorial Timún Más
  Castillejos 294-296, Planta 1a.
  Barcelona 08025, España

Trillas
Editorial Trillas
  Av. Río Churubusco 385 Pte.
  Col.
  Pedro María Anaya Deleg.
  Benito Juárez
  México 03340, D.F., México
  Telephone 688-4233

Foreign Language Specialty Bookstores and Distributors

Adler's Foreign Books
  915 Foster Street
  Evanston, IL 60201-3199
  Telephone (708) 866-6329

AIMS International Books, Inc.
  7709 Hamilton Avenue
  Cincinnati, OH 45231-3103
  Telephone (513) 521-5590

Astran, Inc.
  7965 NW Sixty-fourth Street
  Miami, FL 33266
  Telephone (305) 591-8766

Bilingual Educational Services, Inc.
  2514 S. Grand Avenue
  Los Angeles, CA 90007
  Telephone (213) 749-6213

The Bilingual Publications Company
  270 Lafayette Street, Suite 705
  New York, NY 10012
  Telephone (212) 431-3500;
  (212) 873-2067

Books International
  P.O. Box 27593
  Houston, TX 77227
  Telephone (713) 523-5330

Claudia's Caravan
  P.O. Box 1582
  Alameda, CA 94501
  Telephone (415) 521-7871

Cole-Heffernin Educational Supply
  1001 S. Allen Genoa
  P.O. Box 1717
  Pasadena, TX 77501
  Telephone (800) 448-COLE

DDL Books, Inc.
  6521 NW Eighty-seventh Avenue
  Miami, FL 33166
  Telephone (800) 635-4276

Downtown Book Center, Inc.
  247 SE First Street
  Miami, FL 33131
  Telephone (305) 377-9941

Ediciones del Norte
  P.O. Box A130
  Hanover, NH 03755
  Telephone (800) 782-5422

European Book Company
  925 Larkin Street
  San Francisco, CA 94109
  Telephone (415) 474-0626

Ferndale Books
  P.O. Box 1034
  Ferndale, CA 95536
  Telephone (707) 786-9135

Fiesta Publishing Corp.
  6360 NE Fourth Court
  Miami, FL 33138
  Telephone (305) 751-1181

Follett Library Book Co.
  4506 Northwest Highway
  Crystal Lake, IL 60014

Floricanto Press
  16161 Ventura Boulevard, Suite 830
  Encino, CA 91436-2504
  Telephone (818) 990-1885

French and European Pubns., Inc.
  115 Fifth Avenue
  New York, NY 10003
  Telephone (212) 673-7400

Gessler Publishing Co., Inc.
  65 W. Thirteenth Street
  New York, NY 10011
  Telephone (212) 627-1001

Bernard H. Hamel Spanish Book Corp.
  10977 Santa Monica Boulevard
  Los Angeles, CA 90025
  Telephone (213) 475-0453

D.C. Heath
  125 Spring Street
  Lexington, MA 02173
  Telephone (800) 235-3565

Ideal Foreign Books, Inc.
  132-10 Hillside Avenue
  Richmond Hill, NY 11418
  Telephone (718) 297-7477

Imported Books
  P.O. Box 4414
  Dallas, TX 75208
  Telephone (214) 941-6497

International Book Centre
  P.O. Box 295
  Troy, MI 48099
  Telephone (313) 879-8436

Latin Trading Corp.
  P.O. Box 4055
  Chula Vista, CA 92011
  Telephone (719) 427-7867

Lectorum Publications, Inc.
  137 W. Fourteenth Street
  New York, NY 10011
  Telephone (800) 345-5946

Libreria De La Rosa
  Latin American Imports
  1163 S. King Road
  San Jose, CA 95122
  Telephone (408) 272-1321

Ling's International Books
  7531 Convoy Court
  San Diego, CA 92138
  Telephone (619) 292-8104

Literal Book Distributors
  P.O. Box 713
  Adelphi, MD 20785
  Telephone (301) 445-1041

Mariuccia Iaconi Book Imports
1110 Mariposa
San Francisco, CA 94107
Telephone (415) 255-8193

National Textbook Co.
4255 W. Touhy Avenue
Lincolnwood, IL 60646-1975
Telephone (800) 323-4900

Pan American Book Co., Inc.
4362 Melrose Avenue
Los Angeles, CA 90029
Telephone (213) 665-1241

Puvill Libros
264 Derrom Avenue
Paterson, NJ 07504
Telephone (201) 279-9054

Schoenhof's Foreign Books, Inc.
76A Mt. Auburn Street
Cambridge, MA 02138
Telephone (617) 547-8855

Silver, Burdett & Ginn, Inc.
250 James Street
Morristown, NJ 07960
Telephone (800) 631-8081

Spanish & European Bookstore
3117 Wilshire Boulevard
Los Angeles, CA 90010
Telephone (213) 739-8899

Speedimpex USA, Inc.
45-45 Thirty-ninth Street
Long Island City, NY 11104
Telephone (718) 392-7477

Western Continental Book, Inc.
625 E. Seventieth Avenue, #5
Denver, CO 80229
Telephone (303) 289-1761

Publications Available from the Department of Education

This publication is one of over 600 that are available from the California Department of Education. Some recent publications that relate to the History–Social Science subject area are the following:

ISBN	Title (Date of publication)	Price
0-8011-0913-2	Adoption Recommendations of the Curriculum Development and Supplemental Materials Commission to the State Board of Education, 1990: California Basic Instructional Materials in History–Social Science (1990)	$4.50
0-8011-0689-3	The Blessings of Liberty: Constitutional Teachers' Institute, Final Report (1987)	3.00
0-8011-0874-8	The Changing History–Social Science Curriculum: A Booklet for Parents (1990)	5.00/10*
0-8011-0978-7	Course Models for the History–Social Science Framework, Grade Five—United States History and Geography: Making a New Nation (1991)	7.00
	History Initiative Bookmarks, 1990	6.50/30†
0-8011-0712-1	History–Social Science Framework for California Public Schools (1988)	6.00
0-8011-0892-6	Literature for History–Social Science, Kindergarten Through Grade Eight (1991)	5.25
0-8011-0929-9	Model Curriculum Standards, Grades Nine Through Twelve (1985)	5.50
0-8011-0725-3	Model Curriculum for Human Rights and Genocide (1988)	3.25
0-8011-0968-x	Moral and Civic Education and Teaching About Religion (1991 Revised Edition)	3.25
0-8011-0858-6	Readings for Teachers of United States History and Government (1990)	3.25
0-8011-0672-9	Technology in the Curriculum Resource Materials: Full Package (includes six subject guides and six data diskettes, Data Relator guide and diskette, four 1987 update guides, and the 1988 update) (1986, 1987, 1988)	150.00
0-8011-0675-3	Technology in the Curriculum Update Guides (set of four guides: Language Arts, History–Social Science, Mathematics, and Science) (1987)‡	15.00
0-8011-1016-5	With History–Social Science for All: Access for Every Student (1992)	4.25

*The price for 100 booklets is $30.00; the price for 1,000 booklets is $230.00.
†The price for 100 is $17.50; the price for 1,000 is $145.00.
‡This item is also available in the full package listed above.

Orders should be directed to:

California Department of Education
P.O. Box 271
Sacramento, CA 95812-0271

Please include the International Standard Book Number (ISBN) for each title ordered.

Remittance or purchase order must accompany order. Purchase orders without checks are accepted only from governmental agencies. Sales tax should be added to all orders from California purchasers. Stated prices will be in effect until June, 1992, and include shipping charges to anywhere in the United States.

A complete list of publications available from the Department, including apprenticeship instructional materials, may be obtained by writing to the address listed above or by calling (916) 445-1260.

92 82835

R91-51 (Second printing) 003-0102-91 300 3-92 6,500